QUEEN ESTHER

QUEEN ESTHER

SPIRITUAL WARFARE FROM THE POSITION OF REST

DR. ROTIMI A. OWOADE

CHARIS & GRIT
BOOKS

ISBN: 979-8-90417-223-7

Dedication

I dedicate this book to my wife – Olufunke, and my son, Oluwadamilare, for your unwavering love, sacrifices, and belief in me, even when the journey seemed uncertain.

To my late mother – Deborah Siyanbola, for the foundation of faith and discipline.

And to the One who orders my steps— Jesus Christ, may every word reflect Your purpose.

Preface

In the narrative of Scripture, the story of Queen Esther stands out as a powerful example of faith, strategy, and divine guidance. Her transformation from a Jewish orphan to a key figure in the salvation of her people is not just a historical account; it serves as a blueprint for navigating spiritual challenges with grace, courage, and peace. This book, *Queen Esther: Spiritual Warfare from the Position of Rest*, invites you to explore how Esther's life presents enduring principles for achieving victory in a world filled with unseen battles and divine opportunities.

As believers, we are called to a faith that is both dynamic and purposeful – one that trusts in God's sovereignty while actively participating in His plans. Spiritual warfare is often misinterpreted as a frantic struggle characterized by striving and fatigue. However, Esther's story offers a different perspective: a battle fought from a place of rest, grounded in identity, guided by wisdom, and strengthened by obedience. Her example encourages us to rethink our approach to challenges, blending decisive action with quiet trust, strategic planning with spiritual surrender.

This book is intended for those who wish to walk in victory without sacrificing their peace – for the hidden warriors, the quiet intercessors, and the faithful stewards who feel a divine calling yet seek guidance on how to step into it. Through Esther's narrative, we learn how God operates in the unseen, transforming the ordinary into the extraordinary and empowering His people to change circumstances and rewrite their destinies. Each chapter combines biblical insights with practical applications, providing stories, reflections, and actionable steps to help you integrate these truths into your life.

My hope is that as you navigate these pages, you'll discover the beauty of fighting from a position of victory rather than striving for it. May you find inspiration in Esther's obedience, clarity in her discernment, and strength in her rest. Above all, may you be encouraged to embrace your own "Esther moment," trusting that God has positioned you for this very time. Let her story ignite a renewed passion for partnering with heaven, confidently declaring God's promises while resting in His unwavering faithfulness.

Welcome to a journey of faith, strategy, and triumph. Welcome to the legacy of Queen Esther.

TABLE OF CONTENTS

Preface vii

Introduction: Warfare Doesn't Always Look Like War 1

Overview of Esther's Story 1
Defining "Spiritual Warfare from the Position of Rest" 3
The Unseen Hand of God and Hidden Victories 4

Chapter 1: Chosen in Secret—Identity Before Assignment 7

Esther's Hidden Identity and Humble Beginning 7
Resting in God's Preparation Even in Obscurity 12
Establishing Spiritual Identity as the Foundation of Warfare 16
Living from Identity – The Story of Sarah 21

Chapter 2: The Beauty of Obedience 27

Esther's Willingness to Submit to Mordecai and Hegai's Instructions 27
How Surrender and Humility Precede Spiritual Authority 32
Obedience as a Resting Posture of Trust 36
The Power of Trust: My Reflection 40

Chapter 3: Crowned for a Cause 45

Esther's Elevation to Queen as Divine Positioning 45
Authority Comes from God—Not Striving 48
Resting in God's Placement, Even When You Don't Yet See the Purpose 52
Reflection - Esther's Lesson in Rested Authority 55

Chapter 4: The Hidden War 59

Introduction of Haman and the Spiritual Parallels to Satanic Agendas 59

Warfare Often Begins in the Invisible Realm 63
Rest Means Responding, Not Reacting 67
Responding with Wisdom in a Rushed World – Esther's Way 70
Prayer as the Foundation 71
The Art of Asking Questions 72
Strategic Silence 73

Chapter 5: Fasting for Favor 75

Esther Calls a Fast—Stillness Before Boldness 75
Spiritual Rest Includes Active Surrender 79
Fasting Aligns Us to God's Strategy 83
Fasting for Clarity: A Modern Reflection on Esther's Approach 87

Chapter 6: Bold Moves, Soft Steps 93

Esther Approaches the King With Grace, Not Force 93
Strategic Intercession as Warfare 97
Timing and Wisdom Are Key—God Does More in Stillness Than We Can in Striving 100
Spiritual Boldness in Action: Maya's Story 103

Chapter 7: The Tables Turned 109

Haman's Downfall and the Divine Reversal 109
God's Justice Flows Through Quiet Courage 111
The Power of Standing Still and Letting God Fight 113
Finding Victory Through Stillness – My Reflection 114

Chapter 8: The Decree of Dominion 119

Esther and Mordecai Write a New Decree 119
The Power of Prophetic Declaration and Spiritual Authority 121
Rest Doesn't Mean Silence—It Means Confident Speech 123
Bold Declarations from a Rested Heart – My Reflection 126

Chapter 9: Victory Established 131

The Jews Defend Themselves and Prevail 131
The Outcome of War From Rest: Overwhelming Triumph...133
Learning to Fight From Victory, Not For Victory...................135
Living in Victory – My Reflection..137
Seeing the Victory...139

Chapter 10: Rest as a Legacy 143

The Institution of Purim: Celebration and Remembrance.....143
Rest Is Sustained Through Rhythm, Joy, and Memorials 145
Your Victory Becomes Someone Else's Blueprint 147

Epilogue: The Esther Anointing in Our Time 151

INTRODUCTION

Warfare Doesn't Always Look Like War

...For though we walk in the flesh,
we do not war according to the flesh.

2 Corinthians 10:3

Overview of Esther's Story

When the story of Queen Esther unfolds in the Bible, it doesn't start with a battle scene. There's no clash of swords, no marching armies, and no bloodshed. Yet, beneath the surface lies a deeply strategic and spiritual confrontation—a war waged not with visible weapons but through divine orchestration, wisdom, and quiet courage. Esther's story stands out as one of the most unique expressions of spiritual warfare in all of Scripture, where deliverance comes not through force but through favor, timing, obedience, and a resolute trust in God's unseen hand.

Esther, a Jewish orphan raised by her cousin Mordecai, is suddenly swept into the royal court of Persia. After dismissing Queen Vashti, King Xerxes searches for a new queen. God begins to unfold a hidden plan, which may seem like a random act of royal indulgence. Esther is chosen not just because of her outward beauty but because God's purpose is steering the course of her life.

Her Hebrew name, Hadassah, means "myrtle tree," symbolizing peace and healing in Jewish tradition. Yet, she lives under the Persian name Esther, which can be translated as "star" or possibly linked to the goddess Ishtar. This dual identity reflects the tension in her life—one foot in her Jewish heritage, the other in the complexities of a foreign court. This conflict sets the stage for a divine appointment that would determine not only her destiny but also shape the future of her people.

The political climate was tense, with hidden dangers. Although the Jews had been allowed to return to their homeland after the Babylonian exile, many, like Esther and Mordecai, remained dispersed in the vast Persian Empire. While they lived in peace, their position was precarious. Assimilation was tempting, but their survival depended on maintaining their identity and faith in a God who often seemed silent in the backdrop of pagan rule.

In this environment, Haman, a high-ranking Persian official, rises to power and begins a plot of ethnic cleansing against the Jews, fueled by personal vengeance against Mordecai. The stakes are nothing short of genocide. Yet, the response to this threat doesn't begin with retaliation or resistance. It starts with prayer, fasting, and the humble positioning of a young queen who had been positioned in power "for such a time as this."[1]

Esther's rise to queenship is a plot point and a divine strategy. Mordecai recognizes this and prompts her to understand the spiritual weight of her role. What makes Esther's story distinct is her approach. She doesn't storm into the king's court immediately. She calls for a fast. She waits. She prepares. She moves gracefully and precisely, understanding the delicate balance between boldness and discretion. Each step she takes is a spiritual maneuver, not a human reaction.

---

1 Est. 4:14

This is not a story of overt miracles or thunderous deliverance. God is never mentioned by name in the Book of Esther, yet His presence is unmistakable. Divine fingerprints mark every scene. It's a story of providence disguised as coincidence, of invisible battles, fought through discernment, obedience, and courage.

In the end, Esther does more than save her people. She shifts the laws of the empire, transforms a royal edict, and reclaims territory in the spirit that had been taken in the natural. She does it all not through panic or striving but through deliberate rest, spiritual awareness, and unwavering trust in God's timing. Her life becomes a masterclass in what it means to fight without fighting.

Defining "Spiritual Warfare from the Position of Rest"

To understand the term "spiritual warfare from the position of rest," we must challenge some traditional views of spiritual battle. Too often, warfare is imagined as a frenzied exertion of energy, intense prayer marathons, or endless striving to defeat a seen or unseen enemy. While intercession and spiritual vigilance are biblical, they are not synonymous with spiritual exhaustion. Rest is not passivity. It is a divine strategy.

Spiritual warfare from the position of rest begins with identity. In Ephesians 2:6, Paul writes that we are "seated with Christ in the heavenly realms." This posture is one of authority and stability. A seated position in biblical times indicated rulership, finality, and peace. To be seated with Christ means the war is already won in the heavens; our role is to enforce that victory on earth with wisdom, discernment, and confidence.

Rest is rooted in revelation. It flows from the assurance of who God is and what He has already done. When you know your authority in Christ, you no longer fight for victory—you fight from it. This is the secret Esther tapped into, even if she never used those words. Her fast was not a sign of desperation but of alignment. Her silence was not a weakness but a strategy. Her restraint was not fear but wisdom.

Scripture offers countless examples of this paradox. In Exodus 14:14, Moses tells the Israelites, "The Lord will fight for you; you need only to be still." Jesus, when faced with demonic forces, often cast them out with a word. He did not engage in lengthy rituals. Authority was His default posture. And the same is offered to us.

Rest-based warfare recognizes that not every battle is won by noise. Sometimes, the loudest faith is the quietest resolve. It is the discipline of listening before speaking, of waiting before acting. Esther models this perfectly. She creates moments of pause, moments of space where God can move. She invites divine intervention not by force but by faith.

This posture also dismantles pride. Rest is a declaration that "I trust God more than I trust my effort." In Hebrews 4, the call to enter God's rest is not an invitation to laziness but to obedient faith. It reminds us that striving can become idolatry if it replaces trust. When we lean into rest, we lean into the finished work of Christ.

In spiritual warfare, rest sharpens discernment. When panic clouds our perception, we act hastily. But rest lets us see clearly, move deliberately, and act purposefully. Esther waited three days before approaching the king. That pause changed everything. She gave heaven room to work.

So what does this mean for you? It means battles in your life—whether in your family, career, or personal growth—are not always won by doing more. Sometimes, they are won by knowing more: knowing who you are, whose you are, and where you are seated. When you operate from this position, you war with wisdom, respond with clarity, and rest with power.

The Unseen Hand of God and Hidden Victories

One of the most striking aspects of the Book of Esther is that it never mentions God's name. This omission is not accidental. It invites the reader to perceive God in a different way—through His movements behind the scenes, in the spaces between the words, and in the subtle orchestration of events. It demands a more profound sensitivity to the divine.

From a theological standpoint, Esther reveals the doctrine of providence. God is not absent; He is anonymous. He moves through decisions, dreams, disruptions, and delays. When King Xerxes cannot sleep and orders the royal records to be read, the story of Mordecai's earlier loyalty is brought to his attention. What some might call coincidence, Scripture invites us to call divine coordination.

Hidden victories are not immediately recognized but are no less significant. They are the moments when God shifts an outcome, opens a door, or thwarts a plan without fanfare. In Esther's life, these victories begin when she is selected as queen. They continue when she gains favor with the king. They culminate when Haman is hanged on the very gallows he prepared for Mordecai. Each step feels natural, yet supernatural fingerprints are everywhere.

This is important because many believers today overlook the hidden victories in their own lives. We are conditioned to celebrate only the dramatic breakthroughs. But the Kingdom of God often works in quiet revolutions. The job you didn't get may have spared you future heartbreak. The delayed promotion may have prepared you for a higher calling. The unanswered prayer may be the very thing that protects you.

Recognizing God's unseen hand requires spiritual maturity. It calls us to look beyond the visible, perceive purpose in pain, and discern God's involvement in what others might dismiss. Esther's courage shines in her ability to trust what she could not trace. She risked her life to approach the king without knowing the outcome. Yet behind the scenes, God was aligning every detail in her favor.

Hidden victories also teach humility. When the outcome is clearly the result of God's orchestration and not our own manipulation, we give Him glory. Esther never claims the victory as her own. She continually honors Mordecai, involves her people in fasting, and points the king toward justice.

Your own life likely contains hidden victories. Prayers answered quietly. Doors opened subtly. Battles won without applause. This is how God often works—with precision, not performance. His hand moves history, nations, and hearts in silence. Esther's story reminds us that we do not need visible confirmation to walk in confidence.

Faith, in its purest form, is the ability to see the invisible. Hebrews 11:1 says, "Now faith is the substance of things hoped for, the evidence of things not seen." Esther lived this verse. She stepped into her assignment without a guarantee but with a conviction that God was with her. That conviction changed the world.

The same unseen hand that guided Esther guides you. The same God who orchestrated palace politics to save a nation is moving in your life. Trust that your obedience, prayers, fasting, and quiet acts of faith are accomplishing more than you realize. Rest assured: warfare doesn't always look like war, but victory is always certain when God leads the charge.

CHAPTER 1

Chosen in Secret—Identity Before Assignment

Before I formed you in the womb, I knew you.

Jeremiah 1:5a

Esther's Hidden Identity and Humble Beginning

Esther, a young Jewish girl, lived in Susa, the capital of the Persian Empire—a city of wealth and influence yet also marked by tension and cultural complexity. Her Hebrew name, Hadassah, represented a flowering plant known for its pleasant scent, but the environment she navigated was far from fragrant for a Jewish exile.

Orphaned at a young age, Esther was raised by her older cousin Mordecai. Her upbringing was not glamorous; losing both parents placed her in a vulnerable position within a patriarchal and politically charged society. However, Mordecai took her in, raising her as his daughter and instilling in her their faith and traditions. Her early life was one of quiet development, away from the public eye, where God was already at work, cultivating the qualities she would need for future national deliverance.

Culturally, Esther occupied a unique space. She was a Jew in a Gentile empire, bearing two names: Hadassah, her birth name reflecting her faith and heritage, and Esther, her Persian name, which facilitated her assimilation. This duality was essential to her experience, highlighting the ongoing struggle of navigating identity in a challenging environment. Her Jewish heritage provided her with strength, while her Persian identity granted her access. This combination positioned her for divine intervention.

Every leader chosen by God often emerges from obscurity. Moses was hidden in a basket before becoming a deliverer. David tended sheep before ascending to the throne. Esther's life followed this sacred pattern, where identity is shaped in secret before being revealed publicly. God often conceals His treasures before unveiling them.

During Xerxes' reign, the Persian Empire was expansive, stretching from India to Cush. The palace in Susa was a hub of political power, luxury, and unpredictability. When Queen Vashti refused the king's summons, she was removed from her position, creating an opening in the palace. To fill this vacancy, the empire's officials proposed a beauty contest. The king consented, and a search for the most beautiful young virgins across the empire began.

At first glance, this approach may seem superficial. How could a divine calling emerge from such circumstances? Yet divine strategy frequently utilizes human channels. Esther, an ordinary girl from an exiled minority, was suddenly thrust into the king's harem. She did not volunteer; she was taken. However, in this taking, there was a calling.

Esther concealed her Jewish identity at Mordecai's suggestion. This was not an act of cowardice; it was wisdom. There is a time for revelation and a time for discretion. God often initiates His most significant works behind the veil of anonymity. Esther resided in the palace for months before revealing her true identity. Her assignment was hidden, but her identity remained sacred.

Spiritual identity is not always overt. It is the quiet determination to be who God says you are, even when you cannot declare it publicly.

Esther exemplified this. She did not deny her people but waited for the appropriate moment to reveal her connection to them. Her restraint was not betrayal—it was strategy. This mirrors how God interacts with us. He plants vision and purpose in our hearts but often keeps us hidden until we are ready. That hiddenness is not rejection; it is protection.

There is a powerful lesson here for contemporary believers. Many may feel overlooked, forgotten, or stuck in periods of obscurity. However, in God's kingdom, obscurity is not punishment but preparation. The palace may appear as a promotion, but the true preparation occurred long before Esther entered its gates. Character was developed through quiet obedience, loyalty to Mordecai, and adherence to a faith she could not always practice openly.

Sometimes, the most significant spiritual training occurs in silence. No crowds are cheering, no titles affirming, just God shaping you for something greater. Esther's humble beginnings remind us that influence is often preceded by invisibility.

The king's favor toward Esther was not coincidental. Scripture indicates that she gained favor with everyone who saw her. This was more than mere beauty; it was grace. The Hebrew concept of "Chen" (favor or grace) suggests an anointing that attracts divine outcomes. Esther possessed this favor because she carried God's presence, even in concealment. She did not proclaim her faith; she lived it.

Hegai, the eunuch responsible for the women, took a particular interest in her. He provided her with the best accommodations in the harem, the finest cosmetics, and special attention. This favoritism cannot be attributed to chance. It illustrates the principle that God prepares others to recognize what He has placed in His chosen vessels. Esther did not strive; she rested. Her respectful compliance created alignment. Her humility invited promotion.

In our culture of self-promotion, Esther's story is countercultural. She did not seek attention, assert her rights, or demand recognition. Instead, she followed instructions, respected those in authority, and remained true to her quiet convictions. This positioned her to be chosen by the king—not through manipulation but through divine orchestration.

There is something sacred about being chosen in secret. When God selects someone privately before any public acknowledgment, it fosters depth, builds integrity, and establishes the foundation necessary to bear weight. Esther would later carry the responsibility of an entire nation, but she could only do so because she was first anchored in her hidden identity.

This is a call to modern believers: do not despise the secret places. Embrace the times when no one knows your name. Value the assignments that do not come with applause. Recognize obscurity as a sacred trust. God does not waste silence; He builds warriors in stillness. Esther's anonymity was not a delay; it was her divine training ground.

Often, we desire visibility, assuming that public platforms validate purpose. However, God is more concerned with what occurs when no one is watching. The inner life holds more significance than external accolades. Esther's willingness to be led, listen, and wait became the foundation for her destiny.

Had she entered her assignment prematurely, without maturity, the entire Jewish population might have faced disaster. Timing is crucial. God's delays often reflect His mercy. He matures us in the shadows so we can stand in the spotlight without faltering.

As you reflect on your hidden seasons, consider this: are you allowing God to define your identity before revealing your assignment? Are you cultivating private strength that can support public influence? Are you honoring the Mordecais in your life—those who mentor, challenge, and guide you?

Esther's early obedience to Mordecai was vital. When she entered the harem, she did not choose based on her preferences. She consulted Hegai for guidance and followed his advice. This willingness to submit to process and protocol demonstrated her humility. In God's kingdom, humility always precedes honor.

This message resonates with those who feel caught in between—neither in the fields nor yet in the palace. The space between calling and commission may feel prolonged, but it is not empty. God is at work. He is shaping your voice, your posture, and your discernment. Esther did not rush the process; she trusted it. Through that trust, she was divinely chosen.

It is important to note that Esther was not only physically attractive; she was also spiritually attuned. She recognized the significance of her moment. She understood that influence would carry responsibility and that responsibility would require courage. But before any of this unfolded, she remained hidden—not due to unworthiness, but because she was being prepared.

The Kingdom of God continues to operate in this manner. God selects individuals in secret, nurtures them in obscurity, refines their motives, aligns their hearts, and instills in them a faith that does not rely on public validation. Esther's journey from orphan to queen was not a fairy tale; it was a process of consecration.

Today, we need more leaders willing to be chosen in secret—leaders who don't seek a microphone but carry a mantle; leaders who don't pursue titles but embody truth; leaders who understand that spiritual authority is rooted in identity, not visibility.

Your current season may feel hidden. Your prayers may seem unanswered. Your progress may appear slow. But if God has chosen you, He is preparing you. He is refining your character, strengthening your resolve, and teaching you to trust His timing. Esther's life serves as a reminder that divine selection often begins in quiet places.

When Mordecai instructed Esther to conceal her identity, it was not a compromise of faith—it was a preservation of destiny. There would be a time to speak, but this was a time to listen. There would be a time to reveal, but this was a time to remain silent. The wisdom to discern the difference is a hallmark of maturity.

Before she became a voice for her people, Esther became a vessel for God's plan. That transformation did not occur in a palace; it began in a quiet home with Mordecai, in a world where she was simply

Hadassah. This name, rich with meaning, would remain her anchor even as she wore a crown.

In the eyes of the world, she was an outsider elevated by chance. In God's eyes, she was a chosen vessel prepared in secret. She never needed to announce her identity to wield power. Her life spoke volumes. Her demeanor revealed her position. Her choices reflected her alignment with divine purpose.

The same invitation is extended to you. Will you allow God to define you in secret? Will you embrace the process of being hidden, refined, and strengthened before stepping into your assignment? True power arises not from public platforms but from private consecration.

Remain faithful where you are. Respect those who guide you. Be patient. Esther's life illustrates that God never forgets those He chooses in secret. And when the time is right, He brings them forward—not for fame, but for purpose.

The palace was not Esther's ultimate destination; it was merely her assignment. Her true strength stemmed from her identity prior to becoming queen. Soon, that strength would face challenges beyond her imagination.

As Esther approaches the moment that will transform her life, we recognize that trusting in God's guidance, even in solitude, is not just important—it is vital. A purposeful life begins with a solid, quiet foundation.

Resting in God's Preparation Even in Obscurity

God does not waste periods of silence. The quiet, often overlooked phases of our lives hold more divine purpose than we may realize. For Esther, these hidden years were not lost; they were a time of preparation—the unseen development of a vessel that would one day carry a nation's destiny.

In our modern mindset, we tend to seek visible and measurable progress. Today's culture equates success with movement, results, and recognition. However, the most significant growth often takes place beneath the surface in the Kingdom of God. Just as seeds sprout in darkness before blooming in daylight, Esther's life illustrates this principle with clarity.

She existed in the shadows long before she stepped into the spotlight. Her spiritual foundation was established in the obscurity of Mordecai's household, not in the palace. There were no royal garments, political platforms, or applause. Yet that hidden season was sacred. It shaped her values, discernment, and identity, building within her the quiet strength necessary to carry a heavy assignment.

The urge to rush past obscurity is strong, whispering that you are forgotten, your efforts don't matter, and your purpose has been missed. But God never forgets those He is shaping. The slower the shaping, the stronger the vessel. The deeper the roots, the greater the fruit.

When Esther entered the palace, she embarked on a political and spiritual journey. She underwent twelve months of beauty treatments—six months with oil of myrrh and six months with perfumes and cosmetics.[2] While this may seem like preparation for royal aesthetics, it carries spiritual significance. Myrrh often symbolizes purification, suffering, and consecration in Scripture, while perfumes signify favor and intimacy.

This dual preparation suggests a deeper meaning: a purification of identity and an infusion of divine favor. Esther was not merely being prepared for a king; she was being readied for a pivotal moment. God refined her in private before releasing her in public, and she embraced that process rather than resisting it.

Resting in God's preparation means trusting the gradual work of heaven. It involves believing that silence is not abandonment but alignment. Esther did not clamor for influence or protest the timing. Her posture was one of yielded trust, enabling her to carry authority without arrogance.

Throughout Scripture, we see this pattern repeated. Joseph spent years in prison before rising to power in Egypt. David tended sheep

---

2 Est. 2:12

before becoming Israel's king. Even Jesus spent thirty years in relative obscurity before beginning His three-year ministry. The duration of the hidden season often corresponds to the weight of the assignment ahead.

By resting in God's preparation, we surrender the need to control outcomes. We embrace what the Spirit is doing in the hidden places of our hearts. We stop measuring our worth by visibility and start valuing God's hidden work within us. Esther exemplified this with dignity and grace.

Her restraint was noteworthy. She did not reveal her Jewish heritage or overstep her bounds. She moved with humility, gaining favor not only with Hegai but ultimately with King Xerxes himself. Her rest became her recommendation, and her quiet confidence set her apart from every other woman in the harem.

This kind of rest is not inactivity; it is a spiritual posture. It is a calm resolve anchored in the faithfulness of God. When you know who you are and who has called you, you do not panic when you are not yet seen. You don't strive for a position; you wait for an appointment.

There is a kind of warfare in stillness that resists fear, anxiety, and the urge to self-promote. Esther waged war in her soul by choosing rest over rush, stepping into God's pace rather than her own.

Moreover, resting in God's preparation fosters discernment. Esther knew when to speak and when to wait. That spiritual sensitivity was cultivated not in the throne room but in the waiting room. Her ability to time her request to the king, her wisdom in hosting multiple banquets, and her discernment in approaching Haman were all fruits of a heart trained in the discipline of divine timing.

Many believers today miss the fullness of their assignment because they resist the very season meant to prepare them. We are eager to arrive but hesitant to be refined. Yet, God is not in a hurry. He is more committed to your development than to your deadlines. Esther's obedience in obscurity set the stage for national deliverance.

Preparation also safeguards against premature exposure. Anointing without preparation can be perilous, and influence without integrity is unstable. Esther would eventually stand before the king, risking her life to change the course of history. Had she rushed through the process, she might have lacked the wisdom, humility, and favor necessary for success.

The modern world values visibility, but the kingdom values maturity. It is better to be hidden in God's hand than exposed without His covering. Esther rested in this truth, trusting the unseen work. Consequently, she was not only ready—she was radiant.

Consider how God might be preparing you now. Is there a season you are trying to escape that God is using to shape you? Are you resisting the process meant to strengthen your voice, refine your purpose, and align you with divine timing?

Obscurity is a gift when it comes from God. It shields you from unnecessary distractions, deepens your intimacy with Him, and quiets the noise so you can hear His voice. Esther did not squander her hidden season; she received it as sacred.

Because she honored the hidden place, she carried authority in the public sphere. When her moment arrived, she did not flinch or falter. She rose with boldness, clothed in wisdom, and confident in the God who had prepared her in silence.

We often perceive preparation as skill development. However, in the kingdom, it is also about surrender. Esther surrendered to God's process, refraining from striving for a position or manipulating outcomes. She rested, and her rest became the foundation for her reign.

That kind of rest is a powerful tool. It confounds the enemy, silences fear, and anchors your soul amid storms. Esther's story demonstrates that resting in preparation is not passive; it is actively prophetic. It is a statement of faith that God is working even when we cannot see it.

Every detail of Esther's preparation had a purpose. From concealing her identity to selecting her attire before the king, she moved with intention shaped by rest. Nothing was random; everything was refined.

You may feel unseen, unheard, and overlooked, but you are not forgotten. God is at work, refining your voice, posture, and character. Do not rush the process. Rest in it. Allow God to build what only He can.

In time, like Esther, you will realize that your season of obscurity was not a delay but a divine setup. It was not wasted time but sacred formation. When the moment arrives, you will not only be ready—you will be radiant with the glory of God upon you.

This is not just encouragement; it is strategy. In a world that values speed, rest is a radical act of faith. In a culture of self-promotion, waiting is spiritual warfare. Esther teaches us that sometimes the boldest move is to remain still until God says, "Now."

Therefore, allow the Spirit to speak in your silence. Yield to God's shaping hand. Embrace the preparation you cannot yet understand. Trust that what He forms in secret will be revealed publicly and powerfully.

Ultimately, this leads us to a vital principle: establishing spiritual identity as the foundation of warfare. Esther was not merely prepared to be queen; she was ready to be a warrior. That preparation began by understanding who she was before she knew what she was called to do.

Establishing Spiritual Identity as the Foundation of Warfare

Victory in spiritual battles begins with internal clarity rather than external strategies. Before making declarations, engaging in intercession, or confronting adversaries, it is essential to understand your identity. Esther's strength, authority, and victory were rooted not in her position but in her true self.

Her story demonstrates that power arises from spiritual identity rather than public recognition. Before she could advocate for her people, she needed to discover her voice. While she was known as Queen Esther in the empire, she remained Hadassah within—a woman of the covenant, born from a chosen people.

Identity transcends mere labels; it reflects the spiritual truth of who you are in God's eyes. It influences your thoughts, responses, leadership, and, ultimately, your approach to challenges. Without a solid understanding of your identity, every obstacle can feel like a threat, and every delay can seem like a defeat. However, when your identity is established, battles transform into opportunities, and waiting becomes an act of worship.

Esther operated with spiritual precision because she did not allow her external circumstances to redefine her internal reality. She may have donned Persian garments, spoken the royal language, and resided in a foreign palace, but at her core, she remained connected to her Hebrew heritage and covenant with God. This inner anchor provided her the confidence to make tactical decisions when the stakes were high.

This principle applies to believers today. Effective spiritual warfare begins with knowing who you are in Christ. Your authority stems from your identity as a child of God. Ephesians 1:5 states that we have been adopted into God's family through Jesus Christ. This adoption is both legal and spiritual, granting us access, authority, and alignment with heaven.

Esther did not need to shout to command attention, declare her title to exert power, or stand in her truth to be effective. Her spiritual composure unsettled Haman and garnered favor with the king, ultimately influencing the empire's policies. She did not perform power—she embodied it.

Spiritual warfare involves standing in the light, and light emanates from identity. The enemy's primary tactic is often to create confusion about your identity. If he can instill doubt about your calling, worth, or convictions, he can render you passive. Esther overcame this by remaining grounded in the truth of her origins. She may have been in Persia, but Persia was never in her.

In warfare, clarity of identity stabilizes your stance. It empowers you to speak the truth amid deception, discern when to wait instead of rushing, and anchor your emotions so that fear does not compromise your obedience.

Consider how many biblical figures struggled with their identity before fulfilling their assignments. Moses questioned, "Who am I that I should go to Pharaoh?"[3] Gideon protested, "My clan is the weakest in Manasseh."[4] Even Jesus, before beginning His public ministry, heard the Father affirm, "This is my beloved Son."[5] Affirmation of identity always precedes public warfare.

The enemy often strikes early, attempting to distort your self-image before you step into your purpose. For Esther, this could have manifested as feelings of abandonment, loss, and cultural dislocation. She could have seen herself as a forgotten orphan in a foreign land. Instead, she found quiet confidence in belonging to a people with a promise.

Esther's willingness to risk her life before the king stemmed not from palace training but from spiritual formation. She understood that even if the king rejected her, God would not. This confidence allowed her to approach her destiny with courage rather than hesitation.

In our context, modern believers must root their identity in Scripture, not in career, reputation, or circumstances. You are who God says you are: chosen,[6] dearly loved,[7] seated with Christ,[8] and equipped for every good work.[9] These are not just poetic phrases; they are spiritual realities.

Engaging in spiritual warfare from a place of rest is only possible when identity is firmly established. Rest is not denial; it is rooted in authority. When you know you are a citizen of heaven, you do not panic when challenges arise. When you are confident in your adop-

---

3 Ex. 3:11

4 Judg. 6:15

5 Matt. 3:17

6 1 Pet. 2:9

7 Col. 3:12

8 Eph. 2:6

9 2 Tim. 3:17

tion, rejection no longer defines you. When you are clear about your purpose, delays no longer defeat you.

Esther's example also illustrates that identity must be stewarded. She safeguarded her heritage until the appropriate moment, revealing it neither prematurely nor abandoning it to fit in. Her dual identity required wisdom, and she navigated that balance with grace. When Mordecai urged her to disclose her identity, it was because the moment had come for her identity to align with her assignment.

There is a significant message for those navigating environments that may be hostile to your faith or values. You may find yourself in situations where your beliefs are unwelcome, or your convictions are challenged. Like Esther, you must know who you are, even when you cannot always express it. Your identity should guide your posture, not your visibility.

Spiritual maturity involves discerning when to speak and when to remain silent. Esther exemplified this well. She did not begin her role in the palace with bold declarations; she observed, listened, and waited. When the time was right, her voice carried weight because her life was anchored in truth.

This is the essence of spiritual warfare: you do not dispel darkness through noise but through presence. The presence of someone grounded in identity disrupts the enemy's plans. Esther's mere presence in the palace created a spiritual disruption to Haman's agenda. She did not need to draw a weapon; she simply needed to stand.

Standing is a spiritual act. Ephesians 6:13 instructs us, "Having done all, to stand." Not to run, not to shout, but to stand. This kind of standing is only possible when you are aware of your identity. Esther stood before a king because she had already stood before God in prayer and alignment. Her outward courage was born from inward clarity.

You cannot stand publicly if you have not stood privately. Warfare is not merely confrontation; it is confirmation. It affirms who you are and what you carry. When you understand this, you move with quiet authority. You do not need to prove yourself or strive for recognition; you simply embody who God has made you to be.

This does not imply that the process is easy. Identity is often forged through pressure. Esther faced challenging circumstances: she lived in exile, lost her parents, was taken into the king's court without consent, and faced the threat of death. Yet none of these challenges could erase her identity; rather, they refined it.

Some of your most profound revelations about your identity will emerge during difficult seasons. Adversity reveals what cannot be shaken. If your identity is based on fluctuating circumstances, hardship will destabilize you. However, if it is rooted in eternal truth, no storm can destroy you.

This is the foundation of all spiritual warfare. You cannot fight for your calling if you do not believe you are called. You cannot safeguard your peace if you do not believe you deserve it. You cannot pray with power if you doubt your access to God. Identity precedes authority.

Thus, the first assignment of every believer is not to wage war but to be established. To know your name, source, inheritance, and assignment. Once that foundation is solidified, everything else follows.

Esther was established in secret. She did not receive formal theological training or battle preparation. However, she was trained in her identity. She understood to whom she belonged. This understanding allowed her to respond to crises with composure, resist fear with faith, and transform danger into deliverance.

If you wish to walk in Esther's authority, you must embrace her foundation. Your warfare begins with your identity. Your rest is rooted in knowing whose you are. Your victory is secured not by your strength but by your standing.

Take time today to reaffirm your identity in Christ. Let the Word of God resonate louder than your emotions. Allow the Spirit to confirm what heaven has declared about you. Let the enemy hear the silence of your certainty.

Only then will you be prepared to respond to opposition with calm, rise during crises with clarity, and speak when the moment demands. Esther's identity equipped her for warfare she never formally trained for, and the same can be true for you.

As her moment of destiny approaches, Esther steps forward not as an imposter but as a woman prepared in secret, anchored in her identity, and empowered by heaven. Her next move would not only be personal—it would change the course of history.

This leads us to our next revelation: obedience is not a sign of weakness but a tactical choice. Esther's next powerful weapon is not her words but her willingness to submit. In the upcoming sections, we will explore how the beauty of respectful compliance became the gateway to divine favor.

Living from Identity – The Story of Sarah

Sarah stared at her phone, the glow of the screen casting shadows across her small apartment. Another notification pinged—a colleague's post about a promotion, complete with a curated photo and a caption about "hustling hard." She sighed, feeling the familiar pang of comparison. At 29, Sarah was still piecing together her career, her faith, and her sense of self. The pressure to perform, to prove her worth, was relentless. Yet, something deeper stirred within her—a quiet conviction that her identity wasn't tied to likes, titles, or applause. Like Esther in the Bible, Sarah was learning that her spiritual identity was not just a theological idea but a practical weapon in navigating life's battles.

Sarah's childhood wasn't easy. Raised by a single mother who worked long hours, she often felt like an afterthought, abandoned by a father who left when she was five. Those wounds could have defined her, but Sarah had recently begun attending a small church where the pastor emphasized grounding one's identity in God's Word. "You are chosen," he read from 1 Peter 2:9, "a royal priesthood, God's special possession." Sarah scribbled the verse in her journal, letting it sink in. Like Esther, who refused to let her orphan status dictate her future, Sarah chose to anchor herself in Scripture, not her circumstances. She began reciting daily, "I am God's handiwork, created for good works."[10] These weren't just affirmations—they were truths reshaping her perspective.

At work, Sarah faced constant pressure to compete. Her marketing firm thrived on performance, and her colleagues often angled for attention, embellishing their contributions to impress the boss. Sarah felt the urge to join in, to exaggerate her role in projects to secure a promotion. But she remembered Esther, who didn't vie for the king's favor or manipulate her way into the palace. Esther's rest was her strategy, guided by Hegai's wisdom. Sarah decided to stop performing for validation. Instead, she focused on doing her work well, trusting God's timing. When a major campaign succeeded, she didn't boast—she let her results speak. Her boss noticed, commenting on her quiet confidence. Sarah realized that authority rooted in identity didn't require striving.

In her quieter moments, Sarah was learning to sharpen her discernment. Like Esther, who observed the palace's dynamics before acting, Sarah began pausing before reacting to workplace drama or social media noise. She started scheduling quiet time each morning, praying and listening for God's voice. One day, during a heated team meeting, she sensed an ulterior motive in a colleague's suggestion. Instead of calling it out, she waited, prayed, and later confirmed her suspicion through a private conversation. Her discernment, honed in silence, gave her clarity without confrontation. She was learning that spiritual warfare often required stillness, not shouting.

Sarah also practiced "hiddenness" without losing conviction. At work, she couldn't always quote Scripture, but she embodied its principles—integrity, kindness, and diligence. When a coworker mocked her for declining a shady deal, she didn't waver. Like Esther, who concealed her Jewish heritage but never abandoned it, Sarah carried her faith quietly but firmly. Her convictions shone through her actions, earning respect even from skeptics.

---

10 Eph. 2:10

A mentor from her church, Mrs. Carter, became Sarah's "Mordecai." When Sarah doubted her career path, Mrs. Carter challenged her to trust God's plan. "Pride resists guidance," Mrs. Carter said, "but identity welcomes it." Sarah submitted to her mentor's wisdom, even when it meant stepping back from a high-profile project that felt misaligned. That choice led to an unexpected opportunity—a role that suited her gifts perfectly. Like Esther, Sarah's respect for guidance opened doors her ambition alone couldn't.

Guarding her soul became a priority. The constant noise of news, social media, and office gossip threatened to cloud her peace. Sarah audited her influences, unfollowing accounts that fueled comparison and limiting her news intake. She filled her mind with worship music and Scripture, protecting the gates of her heart. This clarity helped her stay focused, even when workplace politics intensified.

One evening, facing a looming deadline, Sarah felt fear creeping in. She remembered Esther's bold declaration: "If I perish, I perish."[11] It wasn't defeat—it was resolve rooted in identity. Sarah wrote her own declaration: "I am seated with Christ in heavenly places.[12] No pressure can shake me." Speaking these truths shifted the atmosphere. She approached the deadline with peace, delivering her best work without panic.

Sarah learned that identity precedes assignment. She had spent years chasing roles she thought would define her, but burnout followed. Esther waited years for her moment, grounded in who she was before stepping into her purpose. Sarah began focusing on consistency—studying Scripture, praying daily, and building character. When a community outreach project needed a leader, Sarah was ready, not because she sought it, but because her identity was secure.

Her confidence grew, but it wasn't arrogance. Like Esther, who honored the king and Mordecai while knowing her divine purpose, Sarah carried herself with quiet assurance. She didn't need to boast

11 Est. 4:16

12 Eph. 2:6

or prove herself—her confidence came from God's Word, not her achievements. When pressure mounted, she chose rest overreaction. She took breaks to pray, approached challenges deliberately, and found that rest was a powerful response to chaos.

Sarah's journey wasn't perfect, but it was purposeful. She wrote an identity statement, taping it to her mirror: "I am chosen, loved, and equipped by God." She sought Mrs. Carter's counsel regularly, stopped performing for approval, and carved out time for discernment. Like Esther, Sarah moved with intention, grounded in her spiritual identity. She wasn't just surviving life's battles—she was thriving in them, wielding her identity as a weapon of peace, purpose, and power.

Key Takeaways

- **Anchor in Scripture:** Your identity is defined by God's Word, not your past or circumstances.
- **Rest as a Weapon:** Intentional rest brings clarity and strength in spiritual warfare.
- **Submit to Mentors:** Wise counsel aligns you with God's plan.
- **Cultivate Discernment:** Quiet seasons sharpen your ability to see clearly.
- **Declare Truth:** Speaking God's promises shifts your perspective and atmosphere.

Action Steps

1. **Write an Identity Statement:** Use Scriptures like 1 Peter 2:9 or Ephesians 2:10 to craft a personal declaration.
2. **Audit Influences:** Remove media or voices that fuel insecurity or fear.

3. **Schedule Quiet Time:** Spend 10 minutes daily in prayer and listening to God.
4. **Seek a Mentor:** Find a trusted voice to guide your spiritual growth.
5. **Choose Rest:** In one area of pressure, pause and pray before acting.

By living from her identity in Christ, Sarah, like Esther, stepped into her calling with unshakeable peace. Her story reminds us that spiritual warfare isn't about striving—it's about standing firm in who God says we are.

REVIEW REQUEST FOR THE MIDDLE OF THE BOOK

Enjoying this journey with Queen Esther?

If this book has blessed, encouraged, or inspired you, we'd love to hear from you!

Your review helps others discover the message and deepen their own walk of faith.

☞ **Please take a moment to leave a review on Amazon.**

Just scan the QR code below or visit:

Thank you for sowing back into the Kingdom!

CHAPTER 2

The Beauty of Obedience

For this is love for God:
that we obey His commands

1 John 5:3

Esther's Willingness to Submit to Mordecai and Hegai's Instructions

Obedience is one of the greatest strengths in God's kingdom. It requires humility, discernment, and a heart aligned with divine order. Esther's ascent to royalty began not with ambition, but with submission. Her readiness to heed the guidance of Mordecai and Hegai positioned her for extraordinary favor.

Esther's journey illustrates that divine assignments are often initiated through human relationships. God works through people, who frequently carry prophetic significance. Mordecai, who raised Esther after her parents' deaths, was more than just a guardian; he served as a spiritual mentor and a voice of divine alignment. His influence reached far beyond familial ties; it was strategically significant.

When Esther entered the palace and came under Hegai's care, she encountered a new form of leadership. Hegai, although a Gentile and a servant of the Persian court, became a crucial part of her preparation. Esther embraced his guidance, choosing not to insist on her own way but to listen.

The scripture notes, "When the turn came for Esther... to go to the king, she asked for nothing other than what Hegai, the king's eunuch... suggested. And Esther won the favor of everyone who saw her."[13] This verse offers more than just a narrative; it provides tactical information. Esther's restraint and willingness to trust someone more experienced in the palace system set the stage for her divine elevation.

In today's context, submission is often misinterpreted. In a culture that celebrates self-expression and individualism, respectful compliance is mistakenly viewed as a weakness or a loss of agency. However, biblical submission is not about silence or suppression; it is about alignment. It involves recognizing that God frequently communicates through others, and receiving guidance can open the door to one's destiny.

Esther exemplified this truth. She submitted to Mordecai before entering the palace and continued to follow his instructions even after becoming queen. Esther 2:20 states, "Esther had kept secret her family background and nationality just as Mordecai had told her to do, for she continued to follow Mordecai's instructions as she had done when he was bringing her up." This consistency reflects her character.

Consistency in obedience fosters divine trust. God often tests our faithfulness through private submission before granting us public authority. Esther successfully navigated that test. Her commitment to honor Mordecai's counsel demonstrated loyalty and spiritual maturity. She recognized that her position did not eliminate the need for guidance.

---

13 Est. 2:15, NIV

Hegai's role in Esther's preparation is also noteworthy. Although he was not part of her faith community, he possessed valuable knowledge of the palace culture, the king's preferences, and the nuances necessary for advancement. Esther humbled herself to accept his information, choosing not to rely on guesswork or personal preference but to trust the process.

This is a crucial lesson for modern believers: preparation often necessitates submission to those who understand the landscape. Whether spiritual, professional, or relational, God places guides in our lives who possess the insights we need. Ignoring their voices can delay our progress. Esther viewed submission not as subjugation but as a thoughtful approach.

Moreover, her obedience was not blind; it was discerning. She understood when to follow instructions and when to take independent action. When faced with Haman's plot, Mordecai called her to action, but Esther determined the approach: fasting, purposeful timing, and subsequent banquets. This balance between submission and leadership signifies spiritual maturity.

Obedience opened the door to favor but did not undermine Esther's agency; rather, it enhanced it. Because she learned to listen, she knew when to speak. Her practice of submission empowered her to lead with wisdom. Authority without submission leads to rebellion, while authority rooted in yielding to God fosters a lasting legacy.

Esther's cultural context amplifies the significance of her discipline. As a Jewish woman in a pagan empire, surrounded by customs and pressures contrary to her faith, she could have easily assimilated or rebelled. Instead, she chose the path of godly obedience—a route that honored her heritage, respected her mentors, and positioned her for influence.

Her story mirrors the biblical pattern found throughout Scripture. Joseph obeyed in prison before rising to Pharaoh's court. David submitted to Saul's authority despite injustice before becoming king. Even Jesus obeyed the Father in obscurity for thirty years before beginning His public ministry. Obedience is not a detour from destiny; it is the pathway that leads to it.

The practical implications for believers today are significant. Submission to godly mentors, openness to wise counsel, and humility to follow divine guidance are essential disciplines, not optional extras. The favor you seek may be unlocked not through effort but through alignment.

Esther demonstrates that favor follows order. She did not manipulate her way into royalty; she aligned herself with those who understood the process and allowed God to elevate her. Her rise came not from striving, but from yielding to God.

The willingness to submit reflects spiritual maturity. It acknowledges that we do not have all the answers and that God often provides direction through others. It requires strength to yield and vision to recognize the importance of obedience before visibility.

Esther did not disregard Mordecai after becoming queen; she did not outgrow his voice. This humility preserved her legacy. Many forfeit their assignments by ceasing to listen to the voices that shaped them. Esther remained teachable, and her teachability laid the groundwork for her boldness.

Discipline to submit to God's plan is powerful because it aligns us with divine order, producing peace, clarity, and supernatural favor. Esther did not merely follow the rules; she pursued purpose. Her submission was not legalism; it was a spiritual strategy.

A prophetic principle is at play: when you honor the vessels God uses, you honor God Himself. Mordecai and Hegai were instruments carrying wisdom for a season. Esther honored both, thereby respecting the process God had ordained.

Many spiritual battles are lost not due to the enemy's strength but because believers are out of alignment. Disobedience disrupts order, delays timing, and forfeits favor. Esther's story reminds us that spiritual warfare often begins with a yielded spirit.

A yielded spirit is not weak; it is focused. It recognizes the source of help and discerns divine setups in human vessels. Esther listened to Mordecai and Hegai, but ultimately, she was attuned to God through them. This is the essence of obedience: it opens our ears to divine whispers through trusted individuals.

Furthermore, her discipline was timely. She acted without delay, moving forward when prompted. Spiritual procrastination can be as detrimental as rebellion. When Mordecai urged her to approach the king, Esther called for a fast, sought clarity, and proceeded.

Obedience thrives on urgency. It responds to divine calls promptly, as Esther did with immediacy and wisely farsighted thought. This reflects the rhythm of spiritual maturity: rapid compliancy paired with wise execution.

In contemporary discipleship, obedience must be understood in a new light. It is not about hierarchy or blind allegiance; it is about trust in God's voice, timing, and the use of people. Esther trusted Mordecai not because he was perfect, but because he had proven himself faithful.

Identify the voices in your life that offer divine insight. Who has God placed around you to guide your growth? Who can provide correction without causing offense? Esther had Mordecai; discern who your guides are.

Her relationship with Hegai also illustrates cross-cultural humility. Although Hegai did not share her faith, he was positioned to assist her. God can use anyone—even those from unexpected backgrounds—to prepare you for your purpose. Do not overlook divine guidance simply because it comes from unfamiliar sources.

The outcomes of Esther's obedience were remarkable. She gained favor with everyone who saw her, was chosen by the king, and was positioned to rewrite a decree and save her nation. None of this occurred because she forced her way into prominence; it happened because she submitted to God's process.

This is the invitation for every believer: to trust the quiet wisdom of discipline, yield before rising, and listen before speaking. Esther did not start as a queen; she began as a daughter, a disciple, and a vessel in formation.

Obedience shaped her life long before she wore the crown. That same obedience would sustain her when the stakes were high and the cost was life-threatening.

The next section will explore the spiritual dynamics that establish obedience as a gateway to authority. Surrender and humility do not diminish influence; they amplify it. Esther's submission opened doors that no one else could enter. Her subsequent actions demonstrate that surrender is a heavenly strategy.

How Surrender and Humility Precede Spiritual Authority

In the realm of leadership, it's essential to recognize that authority is not solely based on potential. True leadership is granted to those who have been shaped through humility and surrender. These qualities are not merely moral virtues; they are vital for spiritual growth. Esther exemplified this journey into influence, demonstrating that her strength lay not just in her courage or beauty, but in her willingness to trust God. Her humility in a foreign court became the means through which divine authority was exercised on earth.

Surrender involves relinquishing control and consciously choosing to trust in a higher leadership. In spiritual contexts, surrender is a strategic submission to divine guidance. Esther's life illustrates this concept in meaningful ways.

When faced with a national crisis, Esther did not act impulsively. Instead, she chose to lay everything down, asking her people to gather and fast for her. She stated, "Go, gather together all the Jews... and fast for me. Do not eat or drink for three days... When this is done, I will go to the king, even though it is against the law. And if I perish, I perish."[14]

This declaration was not a display of bravado but a profound act of surrender. Esther willingly set aside her personal safety, royal privileges, and status in service of a greater purpose. By humbling herself before her people and inviting their support, she created

---

14 Est. 4:16

space for divine strategy. She also approached the king at the right moment, demonstrating patience and discernment.

This trust in God unlocked her spiritual authority. Before confronting Haman or influencing the king, Esther positioned her heart in submission, aligning herself with divine will. This alignment invited divine intervention, shifting circumstances and revealing hidden agendas. Her authority stemmed not from her title but from her willingness to surrender.

Genuine spiritual authority is not self-proclaimed; it arises from alignment with divine purpose. Esther lacked conventional qualifications for national leadership—she had no formal training in politics or military strategy. Yet she experienced remarkable favor and influence because of her deep surrender.

Humility and surrender are often overlooked in leadership narratives. While the world may celebrate dominance and self-promotion, Scripture offers a different perspective.

Moses became Israel's leader only after decades of preparation in the wilderness. Joseph rose to power in Egypt following years of hardship. David ascended to kingship after serving a jealous Saul with integrity. Jesus, the ultimate leader, demonstrated humility by washing His disciples' feet before facing the cross.

In the kingdom, authority is closely linked to humility. God opposes the proud but extends grace to the humble.[15] He lifts those who submit themselves under His guidance.[16] This principle is non-negotiable.

Esther's humility was active and powerful. She approached every aspect of her mission with reverence, honoring Mordecai, respecting palace protocols, and acknowledging the significance of her situation. She did not act entitled or manipulate outcomes; her influence stemmed from her respect for the process.

---

15 James 4:6

16 1 Pet. 5:6

This spiritual reverence is crucial. Humility is not about devaluing oneself but prioritizing God's will, trusting His timing, and valuing the perspectives of others. Esther exemplified this from the palace to the inner courts.

When she finally spoke to the king, she did so with an invitation rather than a demand. Her request was framed within a relationship, not through rebellion. Because of her respectful posture, her words carried significant weight, leading the king to extend his scepter before she even spoke.

This moment is telling. Authority preceded her words. The scepter symbolized favor, access, and approval—extended not because of her statements but because of the person she had become. She had transformed into a vessel surrendered to divine will, which granted her authority even before presenting her request.

Modern believers must grasp this principle: spiritual authority is not about charisma or platform; it is about alignment. Heaven responds to surrender. When you yield your will to God's, your words gain significance. When you adopt a humble posture, your prayers ascend powerfully.

Humility is strength under control. It rejects entitlement and creates space for divine action. It acknowledges that every opportunity and miracle stems from God's grace, not human achievement.

Esther embodied this understanding, viewing her role as stewardship rather than status. She bore responsibility without allowing it to fuel personal ambition. Her submission was directed toward God, not the approval of others.

Moreover, humility safeguards authority. Pride can distort motives and invite resistance. Esther utilized her position not for self-elevation but to advocate for others, making her platform a space for intercession rather than indulgence. This is why her influence endured.

Every believer is called to adopt this posture. Whether leading a household, business, ministry, or nation, authority must be rooted in listening to God. Without humility, leadership devolves into control;

without surrender, spiritual warfare becomes mere striving. Esther teaches us to lead from a place of humility before seeking authority.

Her story also emphasizes that surrender does not equate to disengagement. It involves thoughtful engagement. Esther acted, planned, hosted banquets, and made decisions, all while maintaining a posture of dependence.

This distinction is vital. The world often urges believers to "take charge," but spiritual leadership starts with "take heed." Following God's plans requires listening before acting, praying before planning, and obeying before responding.

Esther's journey reflects this rhythm:

First, she surrendered: fasting for three days.

Then, she positioned herself: dressing in royal attire and standing in the inner court.

Next, she approached with courage following divine alignment.

Finally, she acted purposefully through banquets and discussions.

Every step was marked by spiritual clarity. There was no reaction, only thoughtful response; no striving, only tactical action; no panic, only purpose. This is the fruit of surrender.

Furthermore, humility fosters teachability. Esther remained receptive to Mordecai's guidance even as her role evolved. She did not allow power to isolate her or influence to render her untouchable. Her humility kept her accountable.

Leaders must resist the urge to outgrow accountability. Authority without accountability can be perilous. Esther embraced both, honoring those who shaped her and remaining open to learning.

This is how God cultivates lasting spiritual authority—not through instant promotions, but through refined postures and private decisions. Authority rooted in humility is unshakeable because it is not born of ambition.

When challenges arise, your posture sustains you. Esther did not falter under the pressure of advocating for her people; her training in surrender had prepared her. Her dependence on God became a way of life, and her humility fortified her strength.

The application for today's believers is clear:

Choose submission to God before seeking visibility.

Choose listening before speaking.

Choose intercession before taking action.

Choose stewardship over status.

These choices may seem slow or unnoticed, but they lay a strong foundation. When crises arise, you will be prepared.

Esther did not suddenly find her boldness before the king; it was cultivated through private surrender. She had already set aside her ego, which is why fear could not restrain her. She was free.

Freedom is the outcome of following God. You are no longer bound by outcomes or paralyzed by opinions. You can act confidently because you are firmly anchored.

God continues to seek individuals like Esther—those who will yield before leading, humble themselves before rising, and serve before speaking. This kind of heart embodies heavenly authority.

Wherever you are positioned, let humility define your approach. Let surrender guide your strategy. Let respectful compliance be your offering. These are not signs of weakness; they are indicators of true spiritual maturity.

As you live from this perspective, you will discover that yielding to God's plan is a powerful tool in spiritual warfare, not just a test of faith. Esther's humble submission became a formidable force against Haman's plans. Her yielded spirit created an opportunity for divine intervention.

This leads to another important teaching: obedience itself represents a posture of rest. From that place of rest, Esther engaged in wise action. She did not strive for victory; she trusted in divine triumph. Her obedience became the link between God's promises and human participation.

Obedience as a Resting Posture of Trust

God invites us to obedience not out of a need for our achievements, but because He seeks our trust. Each act of deference is a statement:

"I trust You more than I trust myself." Esther's approach before the king exemplified not only courage but also a profound sense of peace. Her spirit was anchored in obedience long before she entered the royal court, and from that internal calm, she acted with authority.

Obedience rooted in trust carries a strength that achievement cannot match. Esther's compliance stemmed not from fear of punishment, but from her belief in the wisdom and faithfulness of the One guiding her. When following God is grounded in relationship, it becomes restful.

The discipline Esther demonstrated was not reactive; it was steadfast. She wasn't frantically trying to resolve issues or control outcomes. Instead, she moved in harmony with divine timing, which brought her peace even in dire circumstances.

Trust transforms obedience. It alleviates the pressure to be perfect and replaces it with the serenity of being faithful. Esther's life was not characterized by anxiety or panic; her decisions were marked by precision, timing, and grace. Her rest was not inactivity but a prophetic stillness that signified, "God is already at work. I will move alongside Him, not ahead of Him."

This perspective on obedience is crucial for today's believers. In a world that often values striving, surrender to God becomes a sacred invitation to rest. It is not the absence of action but the presence of divine alignment. When you surrender to God from a place of rest, you are not striving to earn something; you are responding because you already possess it.

Esther understood her favor and anticipated the king's acceptance. This assurance was born not from arrogance, but from intimacy. Her fasting aligned her spirit with God, and her trust quelled her fear. She could approach the king because she had first approached God.

Obedience grounded in rest is not hurried. Esther didn't rush to the king immediately after her fast; she waited for the right moment, sensing the king's openness. Such patience requires trust, affirming that "God's timing is superior to mine."

Her approach was also thoughtful. She didn't present her request in a single conversation; instead, she invited the king and Haman to multiple banquets, allowing God to soften hearts, reveal intentions, and set the stage for a divine turnaround. Obedience from a place of rest recognizes that every step is an act of spiritual warfare.

Esther didn't need to manipulate Haman or accuse him prematurely; she trusted that the truth would emerge at the appropriate time. And it did, because her deference was driven by revelation, not reaction.

Many believers mistakenly equate obedience with doing more, saying more, and proving more. However, Esther teaches us that sometimes obedience involves doing less, speaking little, and allowing God to demonstrate His power.

This does not imply passivity. It requires discernment—waiting for God's direction before moving. Your "yes" should stem from peace rather than pressure.

This approach is countercultural. Most leadership models prioritize productivity, visibility, and urgency. Yet, kingdom leadership begins with trust, which fosters duty that knows when to act and when to wait.

Consider Jesus, who only did what He saw the Father doing.[17] His life exemplified restful obedience. He didn't heal every person or respond to every accusation; He adhered to divine timing with unwavering trust.

Esther mirrored this pattern. Her influence grew because her rest was secure. She didn't bear the burden alone but invited others into fasting and submitted to spiritual preparation, waiting for God's guidance.

Yielding to God as a posture of rest is supported by three core principles: intimacy, clarity, and surrender.

Intimacy nurtures trust. You cannot find rest in someone you do not know. Esther's call to fast was not merely about desperation—it

---

17 John 5:19

was about intimacy, aligning her spirit with God and creating space for communion, from which trust emerged.

Clarity guides timing. Restful obedience does not act impulsively; it waits for clarity. Esther could have exposed Haman at her first banquet, but clarity instructed her to wait. This patience allowed for divine orchestrations that human efforts could not achieve.

Following God brings peace. Esther's declaration—"If I perish, I perish"—was not a resignation but a liberation. She surrendered control over outcomes, finding peace in her deference, which was anchored in faithfulness rather than success.

These three principles provide stability during turbulent times. They keep your spirit calm when chaos surrounds you, transforming obedience from a task into a harmonious rhythm. A rested heart can discern God's voice clearly. It knows when to speak and when to remain silent, recognizing opportunities when they arise. Restful surrender to God leads to fruitful actions.

To embrace this way of living, you must redefine success. Success is not solely about outcomes; sometimes, it is the act of obedience itself. God measures us by our faithfulness, not by results.

Esther's obedience led to national deliverance, but that was not her guarantee; it was God's reward. Her responsibility was to obey, while the outcomes belonged to heaven.

This perspective shifts how you pray. Shift from pleading to aligning. It also reshapes your leadership as you move from abundance. You don't seek validation; you walk in affirmation. Your leadership becomes prophetic, flowing from a place of peace.

Esther's leadership was honed in rest. She influenced a king, reversed a genocidal decree, and secured a lasting legacy, all beginning with stillness rather than strategy.

Obedience as rest quiets the clamor of comparison. Esther was not competing with others for attention; she focused solely on God. Because she obeyed Him, favor followed her.

You do not need to announce your presence when you are aligned with God. The anointing will create opportunities for you. Favor will find you, and doors will open as heaven permits.

This occurs only when trusting God is your default and trust is your foundation.

In a culture that rewards urgency, obedience rooted in rest will distinguish you. It may confuse others and appear inefficient, yet it will yield results that striving cannot achieve.

Esther's rest provided her with strategy, her strategy led to impact, and her impact created a legacy. It all began with trust.

When obedience becomes rest, warfare transforms into worship. Your actions emerge from presence, not pressure. Your strategies are born from prayer, not panic. Your influence becomes unstoppable, manifesting first as invisible before it becomes undeniable.

The rest you seek is found not in escape, but in obedience. This obedience is not a performance; it is a relationship.

Like Esther, you are called to more than mere survival. You are called to stewardship, influence, and spiritual authority. Yet, this journey does not start with striving; it begins with rest.

As we examine the practical applications of this principle, we can observe how Esther's quiet surrender exemplifies a pathway to achieving remarkable breakthroughs. Her obedience was not merely a personal quality, but a strategic asset. From this, we will derive practical illumination into embracing a life of obedience as a natural expression of trust.

The Power of Trust: My Reflection

In the chaos of my overcommitted life—balancing a demanding job, family responsibilities, and the constant hum of notifications—I found myself craving clarity. Decision fatigue had become my unwelcome companion, and I longed for a way to align my choices with something greater than my own fleeting instincts. That's when I stumbled back into the story of Esther, a woman whose life wasn't defined by her crown but by her quiet, intentional obedience. Her story wasn't just a dusty biblical tale; it was a roadmap for navigating my modern mess with trust and purpose.

Esther's obedience wasn't reactive or fear-driven—it was a deliberate choice rooted in trust. She didn't just follow orders; she leaned into God's timing, trusted the voices He placed in her life, and surrendered her need for control. Her life offers a framework for any believer, whether you're a corporate professional, a stay-at-home parent, or someone wrestling with a calling that feels bigger than your courage. Here's how her example became my guide—and how it can become yours.

Staying Teachable in the Midst of Influence

I used to think that once I reached a certain level of success, I wouldn't need mentors anymore. But Esther, even as queen, honored Mordecai's guidance. She stayed teachable, recognizing that submission to godly voices wasn't a sign of weakness but a structure for growth. In my own life, I started seeking out mentors again—not to control me, but to cover my blind spots. I began to see correction as protection, not punishment. Whether it's a pastor, a trusted friend, or a colleague with wisdom, staying teachable keeps us aligned with God's path. Ask yourself: *Are there voices in my life I need to listen to more closely?*

Embracing the Process, Step by Step

Esther spent twelve months in preparation under Hegai's guidance, trusting the process instead of rushing to the throne. I'm guilty of wanting to skip steps—craving the promotion, the platform, or the breakthrough without the character-building grind. But Esther's story reminds me that God's preparation is never wasted. Instead of asking, "When will I be seen?" I've started asking, "What is God forming in me right now?" Every act of obedience in the unseen seasons plants seeds for future authority. Embrace your current season, whether mundane or challenging and trust that God is shaping you for what's next.

Listening to the Right Voice at the Right Time

When the crisis hit, Esther didn't react to the noise of the crowd—she tuned her ear to Mordecai's prophetic urgency and responded with her own Spirit-led strategy. In my life, I've learned to filter out voices driven by drama and seek those grounded in discernment. Before making big decisions, I now pause to pray and, when needed, fast. Esther's example shows obedience isn't about waiting for perfect conditions but acting swiftly and wisely when God speaks. *What has God asked you to do recently that you've delayed?* Confirm His voice through prayer, then move with courage.

Trusting Without Needing the Full Picture

Esther's bold declaration, "If I perish, I perish," wasn't reckless—it was a surrender to God's plan without demanding guarantees. I've spent too many nights wrestling with the need for control, wanting God to show me the entire map before I take a step. But Esther's trust taught me that obedience doesn't require clarity on the outcome—just faithfulness at the moment. Letting go of the "why" and embracing the "what" brings a surprising rest to the soul. Trust says, "God sees the full picture. I only need to say yes to my part."

Anchoring Obedience in Prayer and Fasting

Esther didn't act in her own strength; she called for a fast, aligning her steps with heaven's strategy. I've started incorporating fasting into my decision-making, not as a ritual but as a way to clear distractions and hear God's timing. Before a major career move last year, I fasted for three days, and the peace that followed was undeniable. Obedience flows best when rooted in intimacy with God. *Is there an area in your life where fasting could bring clarity?*

Moving with Grace, Not Force

Esther approached the king with dignity and timing, not manipulation or haste. Her obedience was bold yet gentle, creating space for hearts to shift. I've learned to replace frantic striving with grace-filled steps—whether it's addressing a conflict at work or making a request at home. Spiritual urgency without divine timing leads to strain, but obedience led by the Spirit produces results with peace. Let your words and actions reflect trust, not tension.

Choosing Calling Over Comfort

Esther could have stayed silent and safe in the palace, but she chose God's call over her comfort. When asked to lead a project that felt beyond my expertise, I faced a similar moment. Staying in my comfort zone was tempting, but Esther's courage pushed me to say yes. Obedience often costs something—popularity, ease, or even security—but it never costs intimacy with God. *What comfort zone are you being asked to leave?* The obedient rises, even when it's inconvenient.

Rooting Obedience in Identity

Esther didn't obey to earn favor; she obeyed because she knew who she was in God's eyes. When I began seeing myself as a child of God, not a performer, obedience became less about pressure and more about love. It's not about striving for approval but resting in identity. This shift—from fear-driven compliance to identity-driven obedience—brings peace and confidence. When you know who you are, yielding to God's plan becomes natural.

Tracking the Fruit of Obedience

Esther's obedience saved a nation, a ripple effect she couldn't have predicted. I've started journaling the outcomes of my own steps of faith—breakthroughs, divine connections, even small confirmations. Last month, obeying a nudge to reach out to a struggling colleague led to a conversation that shifted their perspective. Tracking these moments fuels my faith for the next step. *Keep a record of what follows your obedience.* It's a reminder that surrender to God is never wasted.

A Call to Action

Esther's life shows that obedience isn't a performance—it's a partnership. It's not about striving for outcomes but resting in God's plan. This week, I challenge you to:

- Write down one area where obedience feels hard.
- Find a Scripture that speaks to that area.
- Declare your trust in God and take one actionable step.
- Share your journey with a mentor or friend.
- Journal the fruit that follows.

As I've leaned into Esther's model, I've found rest in my soul, clarity in my decisions, and alignment with God's path. Her crown wasn't the goal; it was a tool. Her obedience wasn't a burden; it was a bridge to purpose. In a world that screams for control, Esther's trust invites us to rest, obey, and watch God transform our steps into something eternal.

CHAPTER 3

CROWNED FOR A CAUSE

...Yet who knows whether you have come to
the kingdom for such a time as this?

ESTHER 4:14B

Esther's Elevation to Queen as Divine Positioning

From an outside perspective, Esther's promotion appeared to stem from her charm, elegance, and favor with the king. However, behind the scenes, God's influence was at work. Long before Haman's plot unfolded, God had prudently placed a Jewish woman in a significant role within the Persian empire. Her rise was not for her own benefit; it served a greater purpose.

This perspective shifts how we understand success and promotion. In God's economy, elevation is never about personal comfort; it is for a higher calling. Esther illustrates that divine positioning often comes with hidden responsibilities. The palace was not the end of her journey; it was the platform for her next level of yielding to God.

God's sovereignty is evident throughout Esther's rise. Every detail—from Vashti's removal to Hegai's favor to the king's decisions—was part of a larger plan. Esther did not create her opportunity;

she did not manipulate her way to power. Instead, she stepped through the doors God opened with grace and trust.

The essence of spiritual elevation lies in divine orchestration, not self-promotion. Too often, individuals are tempted to pursue platforms instead of preparing for their purpose. Esther reminds us that when God opens a door, it is a setup for something greater.

Promotion in the kingdom comes with responsibility. Esther did not receive a crown for luxury; she was given it to be a voice for the voiceless. Her position at the royal table was not about her comfort but her capacity to intercede and take action.

When Mordecai reached out to Esther about Haman's decree, his words cut through the illusion of safety: "Do not think that because you are in the king's house you alone of all the Jews will escape. For if you remain silent at this time, relief and deliverance for the Jews will arise from another place... And who knows but that you have come to your royal position for such a time as this?"[18]

This statement shifted Esther's perspective, awakening her to the reality that her position had a purpose. Her crown was not merely for adornment; it was a tool for action. Her influence was not a reward; it was a responsibility.

This principle applies to every believer. Wherever God has placed you—be it in business, ministry, education, government, or home—you are there for a reason. You are positioned for influence and called to intercede. Your crown represents your calling.

The challenge is to avoid separating our faith from our position. Esther could have chosen this path. She could have remained silent, detached, and hidden. However, Mordecai's words ignited something within her, dispelling the notion that her elevation exempted her from responsibility. They reminded her that purpose always surpasses self-preservation.

Many believers today hold positions of influence yet remain unaware of their assignments. Esther teaches us that the crown is just the beginning. It is not the end goal; it is the means to fulfill a mission.

---

18 Est. 4:13-14

So, what does it mean to be crowned for a cause?

It means viewing your position through the lens of purpose.

It means refusing to settle for influence without intercession.

It means recognizing that visibility is not the goal—it is the gateway.

Esther's response was courageous. She embraced the weight of her role and chose to act, even at the risk of her life. Her transformation from passive royalty to active assignment elevated her from a queen by title to a queen by function.

You may not wear a literal crown, but you carry the authority of the King. You are seated with Christ in heavenly places.[19] Your workplace is not just a job; it is a divine appointment. Your influence is not random—it is essential.

Esther's story serves as a call to action. It reminds us that we were not saved to be safe; we were positioned to be powerful, and true power flows not from status but from surrender.

The beauty of divine positioning lies in God's ability to use ordinary people to achieve extraordinary outcomes. Esther was not born into royalty; she was a Jewish orphan in a foreign empire. But God recognized her, prepared her, and utilized her when the time was right.

Your past does not disqualify your purpose, and your limitations do not negate your calling. When God crowns you, it is because He trusts you with a cause.

The enemy may try to convince you that you are merely in the palace to survive. However, heaven declares that you are there to intercede, advocate, and activate change.

So, consider these questions:

- What environment has God placed me in that needs a voice of righteousness?
- What opportunities has God opened that require more than mere presence—they require purpose?

---

19 Eph. 2:6

- What gifts has He given me that I may have hidden, thinking they were unnecessary in this season?

Esther's example calls for a response. She challenges us to stop playing small, to stop compartmentalizing faith and influence, and to stop viewing elevation as the ultimate goal. Instead, we should see the crown as a call—a call to intercede, a call to speak, a call to act.

By following Esther's example, we discover that true authority comes not from our position in the palace, but from our place in God's plan. Her crown did not change who she was; it revealed who she had always been. Now, that same invitation is extended to us: to rise, reign, and recognize that we, too, have been crowned for a cause.

Divine positioning becomes even more impactful when we understand the source of our authority—not through striving, talent, or effort, but through God Himself. This leads us to the next revelation in Esther's journey: that authority comes from God—not from personal ambition. Her rest, wisdom, and strategy all stemmed from divine appointment, not self-driven goals.

Authority Comes from God—Not Striving

Power in the Kingdom of God is not driven by personal ambition. Authority is not earned through effort or claimed through charisma; it is granted. True authority is bestowed from above, not created from within. The life of Esther exemplifies this principle in Scripture. She did not fight her way to the throne; she was chosen, and that choice came with divine authority.

From her modest beginnings in Mordecai's household to her elevation in the palace, Esther never sought to be at the center of power. She did not pursue influence. Instead, she walked through the doors that God opened, never forcing outcomes. Each step she took was characterized by discernment, restraint, and responsiveness to divine timing. Her journey challenges our cultural fixation on relentless striving.

We live in a society that idolizes hustle. The louder the voice, the better. The busier the individual, the more successful they appear. The more assertive, the more powerful. Yet, Scripture presents a different perspective. Authority flows through humble vessels, not aggressive personalities. It comes from those who recognize that favor cannot be manufactured, and that spiritual power arises from posture, not performance.

Esther wore her crown with grace, not arrogance. She did not wield it as a tool for dominance but as a platform for obedience. Aware of the sacredness of her role, she understood that her assignment was from God, and thus, only He could sustain her authority.

When standing before the king, she spoke with calm assurance. She did not over-explain or compensate. Instead, she stood, waited, and trusted the God who had placed her there. This exemplifies spiritual authority: confidence without arrogance, boldness without desperation.

As Paul noted in Romans 13:1, "There is no authority except that which God has established." This principle applies not only to civil governance but also to spiritual structure—authority, whether natural or spiritual, is granted by God. No amount of striving can replace divine placement.

Esther found herself in a position of influence because God had predetermined it. While the process may have appeared political to observers, it was prophetic from heaven's perspective. God positioned her before the crisis arose, preparing her for a battle she was unaware of.

This understanding liberates believers from the trap of striving. Recognizing that authority is granted, not seized, allows you to rest in God's providence. You stop comparing your timing to others, stop pursuing what hasn't been assigned to you, and begin focusing on stewardship rather than status.

Esther's life illustrates that true authority does not need to be asserted. She never proclaimed her influence; her mere presence held weight because she was aligned with heaven. Her silence was tactical, and her few words were powerful. This is the essence of real authority: it does not need to prove itself.

Jesus embodied this truth as well. He did not strive for status. Philippians 2:6-7 states that "being in very nature God, He did not consider equality with God something to be used to His advantage; rather, He made Himself nothing by taking the very nature of a servant." What followed? God exalted Him. Authority flowed from humility.

Many leaders experience spiritual exhaustion from trying to manufacture influence. They overlook that striving depletes, while surrender replenishes. Esther avoided this pitfall. She did not compete for position; she prepared quietly, acted when prompted, and God magnified her influence in due time.

Rest becomes attainable when you understand the source of your authority. If God granted it, only He can sustain it. If He has not yet given it, no effort will yield fruit.

Esther's strategy began with her recognizing her role in the divine narrative. When Mordecai informed her of Haman's genocidal plot, she did not panic or rush to the king uninvited. Instead, she called for a fast, paused, and waited. This was not a sign of weakness but of authority guided by wisdom.

Too often, we equate activity with authority. Yet, restraint can signify greater power in God's kingdom. Esther fasted before taking action. She consulted heaven before confronting her adversary. Because she trusted God, she did not need to manipulate outcomes.

Spiritual authority is about alignment. Esther did not shout to make her case. She whispered purpose into a receptive heart. Her words carried weight because her spirit was at peace.

Leaders across all sectors—ministry, business, government, or family—should learn from Esther. Cease striving and begin stewarding. Stop forcing and start flowing. Authority arises when you fulfill your role without idolizing the outcome.

If your assignment is from God, it is protected by Him. Esther's life demonstrates that divine authority comes with divine protection. Haman's plot could not succeed because God had already placed Esther. She did not need to rush or defend herself; she simply needed to show up, speak the truth, and let God work.

One remarkable aspect of Esther's authority was its quietness. There was no political spectacle, no rebellion, no manipulation—just quiet courage that made a significant impact. That is the kind of authority that God honors.

So, what can believers learn from this?

1. **Stop Competing.**
   Authority is not a race. Your timeline is not delayed because someone else has advanced. God has a specific assignment for you that no one else can fulfill.
2. **Clarify Your Assignment.**
   Striving often stems from confusion. When you lack clarity on your purpose, you may reach for roles that do not belong to you. Ask God: What have You called me to carry in this season?
3. **Align With Heaven's Timing.**
   Rest does not equate to inactivity. It means being responsive. It involves waiting for God's go-ahead before taking action. Esther waited, then she moved.
4. **Stay Rooted in Humility.**
   You do not need to promote yourself when God is your promoter. Let humility guard your heart so that authority flows from purity.
5. **Minister From Overflow, Not Emptiness.**
   Striving drains energy. Rest rejuvenates. Authority flourishes when your private time with God fuels your public influence.

There is a unique peace that comes from knowing your authority does not rely on your own efforts. It liberates you from perfectionism and prevents burnout. It empowers you to say no when necessary and yes without fear.

Esther had nothing to prove; she only needed to be faithful. Because she understood the source of her authority, she used it wisely. Her influence transformed a death sentence into deliverance. Her restraint became her strength, and her timing saved a nation.

This is not merely a story about a woman who became queen; it is a strategic guide for anyone who wishes to lead with heavenly authority.

Rest is the foundation. Trust is the compass. Surrender to God's plan is the map. And God is the one who opens every door.

Take a step back, breathe, and stop forcing doors to open. Ask the Spirit, "Where have You already entrusted me with responsibility?" Steward that and walk in it.

When you cease striving and begin trusting, your impact multiplies, and authority flows through you rather than being something you pursue.

This leads us to a powerful truth in Esther's story: even when you do not fully understand why you were positioned, resting in God's placement allows Him to reveal His purpose. This is the essence of the next revelation in her life—**resting in God's placement, even when you do not yet see the purpose**.

Resting in God's Placement, Even When You Don't Yet See the Purpose

Divine placement can often feel unclear or even arbitrary. However, God always has a purpose when He places someone in a position. For Esther, her crown was established before the crisis, and her throne was secured before the threat emerged. She was in her role long before she fully grasped its significance. This highlights an important spiritual principle: God positions us before revealing our purpose.

Finding peace in that placement, even when the purpose is not evident, serves as both a test and a calling. Esther navigated the challenge of being elevated without explanation. For a time, her life in the palace seemed disconnected from her Jewish identity and any larger mission. Yet, in that silence, God was crafting a story.

There is a divine strategy in waiting. This is not a passive delay; it is a protective concealment. God often hides His people in plain sight while preparing something significant. Esther was not idle in her assignment; she was being shaped by it. Her development required trust in the God who saw what she could not.

Many believers today grapple with the in-between—caught between calling and clarity. Like Esther, they find themselves placed but not yet purposed, elevated but not yet activated. This space is sacred, teaching faith that does not depend on visibility and inviting rest in God's sovereign will.

Esther had to trust that her story was not random. She needed to be assured that the same God who brought her to the palace had a purpose for her placement. This rest was not laziness; it was spiritual composure—the ability to be present without needing all the answers.

The modern church often equates movement with meaning. We feel valued when we are busy and validated when we are seen. However, in God's design, hiddenness can be just as holy as promotion. Embracing your current placement means accepting the role you've been given, even if it seems unremarkable or disconnected.

Esther's ascent to the throne was not linked to immediate action. She did not enter leadership by launching a campaign; she did so through obedience and patience. Her strength came not from being loud but from being available.

This posture of rest requires surrender. It means letting go of the need for constant understanding and trusting that God's timing is perfect and His placement intentional. Esther did not have the benefit of hindsight; she woke up each day in the palace, waiting for a reason.

When the moment arrived—when Haman's decree threatened her people—she understood. The years of waiting were not in vain. The silence had a purpose, and her placement held prophetic significance.

The same applies to you. You may feel hidden or question your current situation. But God does not make mistakes. Every placement is preparation. Every season shapes you. Every role refines you. Resting in your placement requires spiritual discipline. You must guard against comparison, resist the urge to force significance, and learn to see beyond the surface.

Esther was not in the palace due to her ambition but because of her assignment, which would unfold over time, through testing and tension. She remained where God had placed her until the right moment came. When Mordecai informed her of Haman's plot, Esther could have reacted with panic or pride. Instead, she responded with perspective, recognizing her placement as a calling rather than a coincidence.

The palace was not a reward; it was a role that required readiness. Readiness is cultivated in rest. Rest is not inactivity; it is active trust and spiritual alertness without anxious striving.

In times when you cannot see the reasons, focus on the who. Who placed you? Who sustains you? Who is working behind the scenes? Esther anchored her identity in the God of her people, even when His name was not mentioned in the palace.

This kind of faith does not define success by visibility. It finds fulfillment in following God and views placement as sacred, even before the assignment is clear.

Are you content with where God has placed you? Are you seeking a platform or listening for guidance? Have you mistaken inactivity for insignificance?

Esther's life teaches us that being placed is part of the process. You may not always choose your placement, but you can choose your attitude within it. Esther chose humility, discretion, and honor.

These choices are available to you as well. In your workplace, home, and ministry—wherever you are—you can find peace in knowing that God is not confused about your location. He has planted you, and where He plants, He provides.

You do not need a complete plan to walk in full faith. You only need to trust the One who holds the blueprint. Esther did not see the end when she entered the palace, but she remained present, faithful, and positioned.

When God's purpose was finally unveiled, she was ready. She did not need to rush to catch up; her readiness stemmed from her rest.

Let this be an encouragement: do not despise your placement, do not rush through the waiting. Trust God's plan. Your present placement holds unseen sacredness. There are people only you can reach, rooms only you can access, and assignments only you can fulfill.

Sometimes, the most spiritual thing you can do is stop striving to be elsewhere. Be present. Be available. Be faithful. Esther's willingness to stay made her available when it mattered. Her consistency made her trustworthy when it counted.

If you find yourself in a season of hiddenness or perceived irrelevance, remember Esther. She was placed before she was purposed and seated before she was sent. Her rest did not delay her destiny; it positioned her perfectly.

So, stand firm. Stay faithful. Watch God work. He has placed you with purpose, and your assignment is closer than you think.

As we move into the next chapter of Esther's story, her settled placement begins to yield results. In the next phase, her rest transforms into revelation, and her strategy becomes supernatural. But it all starts here—with the rest of someone who knows she is right where God wants her to be.

Reflection - Esther's Lesson in Rested Authority

In a world obsessed with hustle, where ambition is a badge of honor and visibility is currency, the story of Esther feels like a quiet rebellion. Her rise to influence as a queen in ancient Persia wasn't the result of self-promotion or relentless striving. It was the fruit of something deeper—a spiritual posture rooted in humility, patience, obedience, and rest. Esther's life reframes how we think about power, placement, and divine timing, offering a blueprint for believers today to cultivate a kind of authority that doesn't demand attention but receives it through alignment with God's purpose.

I remember a season in my own life when I felt stuck in a job that seemed insignificant. I was a junior analyst, crunching numbers in a cubicle, while my peers seemed to be climbing corporate ladders or launching passion projects that lit up social media. I craved recognition, a platform, anything to prove I was "called" to something greater. But Esther's story challenged me to see my placement differently. She wasn't in King Ahasuerus's palace because of ambition or coincidence. God had positioned her there, not just for her own sake but for a purpose that would unfold in divine timing. Like Esther, I had to learn that I wasn't misplaced—I was positioned. The question wasn't "Why am I here?" but "What is God preparing me for?"

Discerning the Purpose of Your Placement

Esther's story begins with her placement in a seemingly impossible context—a Jewish orphan in a Persian palace. Yet, she didn't resist her circumstances or demand clarity. She accepted her place as intentional, trusting that God had a reason for it. Today, we can ask the same questions: Who's around me that needs my influence, compassion, or advocacy? What problem in my sphere might God want to solve through me? At my old job, I started noticing the people around me—a coworker struggling with anxiety, a manager who needed encouragement. These were clues to my assignment. When we discern divine purpose in our location, we stop waiting to be "used" and start walking as one already sent.

Letting Authority Find You

Esther didn't lobby for the throne or chase the crown. She was chosen, not because she demanded attention, but because she rested in God's selection. This is countercultural in an age where we're told to build our personal brand or seize opportunities. I once spent months networking, trying to prove my worth to leaders who barely noticed me. Exhaustion set in until I realized that spiritual authority doesn't come from striving—it comes from surrender. Letting go of the need to prove your calling, as Esther did, frees you to lean into your assignment, even if no one sees it yet. Heaven notices your obedience, and when God is ready, the crown will come—and it will fit because you were already prepared.

Embracing Hiddenness and Preparation

The months Esther spent in the palace before the crisis weren't wasted. They were a season of hiddenness, where her character was forged, her discernment sharpened, and her spiritual awareness deepened. I've learned not to dismiss what looks like inactivity. In my cubicle days, I studied leadership books and prayed for wisdom, not knowing how God would use it. Hiddenness is where roots grow deep, making you unshakable when your moment arrives. Esther's twelve months of preparation, without knowing the full goal, teach us that faith isn't passive—it prepares. Whether it's learning a skill, studying Scripture, or building relationships, preparation without clarity is a test of trust, and trust is the currency of spiritual authority.

Rest as Spiritual Warfare

When crisis hit, Esther didn't react impulsively. She fasted, prayed, and rested in God's timing, creating space for divine strategy. This kind of rest isn't disengagement—it's warfare. It resists fear, steadies emotions, and sharpens discernment. I've practiced this by setting aside one day a week to fast from decision-making, simply praying and listening. It's remarkable how clarity emerges when you refuse to act on impulse. Rest confuses the enemy and aligns you with God's pace. Esther's stillness before approaching the king wasn't weakness; it was wisdom.

Stewarding the Crown, Not Worshiping It

When Esther became queen, the crown wasn't her goal—it was her tool. She used her position to save her people, not to bask in glory. Too often, we idolize platforms, chasing followers or titles while forgetting their purpose. As God entrusts us with influence, we must ask: What am I meant to build with this authority? Who am I called to serve? Esther's favor was sacrificial, tied to the legacy of her people. Whatever God places in our hands—a team, a family, a network—isn't just for us. It's for those He wants to reach through us.

Staying Open to Truth

Esther's openness to Mordecai's counsel kept her grounded. She didn't isolate herself in her royal identity; she listened to voices outside her echo chamber. Modern leaders need this humility—keeping spiritual mentors, inviting feedback, and listening for God's whispers in unlikely places. I once ignored a mentor's advice, thinking my new role made me untouchable. I stumbled until I learned that elevation increases our need for correction, not diminishes it.

Aligning Habits with Purpose

Esther's wisdom wasn't a one-time act; it was a lifestyle. She walked in discernment long before her defining moment. Similarly, resting in God's placement is a daily discipline. I start each day with Scripture, dedicating my plans to God. I organize my week to steward time and relationships intentionally, setting goals that reflect surrender rather than hustle. This rhythm turns rest into readiness, preparing us for the moment God calls us to act.

A Call to Rested Authority

Esther's story isn't just history—it's a challenge. Spend 30 minutes reflecting on where rest is hardest for you. Ask God to reveal how striving might be clouding your purpose. Confess the need for control and write a statement of trust for your current season: *"I trust that God has placed me here for a purpose, and I will rest in His timing."* Share it with a friend for accountability. Practice spiritual disciplines like daily Scripture meditation, weekly fasting, or monthly prayer retreats to anchor yourself in God's pace.

Esther's authority was born in rest, confirmed in trust, and multiplied in crisis. She didn't force her way into her calling; she aligned with it. Her story reminds us that we don't need to seize power to walk in it. If God has placed you, He will reveal why. Your job is to stay ready, humble, and in rhythm with Him. As Esther's next chapter unfolded, her rest became the foundation for discernment, and her placement became a launchpad for invisible warfare. Spiritual authority doesn't always look like a sword—sometimes, it looks like stillness, poised for the moment God moves.

CHAPTER 4

The Hidden War

For we do not wrestle against flesh and blood, but against principalities, against powers, and against the rulers of the darkness of this age, against spiritual hosts of wickedness in the heavenly places.

Ephesians 6:12

Introduction of Haman and the Spiritual Parallels to Satanic Agendas

Haman's lineage traces back to the Amalekites, longstanding adversaries of Israel. The Amalekites were the first to assault Israel after their exodus from Egypt.[20] God declared perpetual enmity against Amalek for attacking the vulnerable from behind. King Saul's failure to eliminate King Agag, an Amalekite, resulted in the prophet Samuel executing him. Generations later, Haman—a descendant of Agag—ascends to power in the Persian Empire. This situation transcends mere politics; it reflects prophecy.

20 Ex. 17:8-16

Esther's narrative illustrates how ancient spiritual conflicts often resurface in contemporary contexts. Haman's animosity towards the Jews is not personal; it stems from a broader, malevolent agenda. When Mordecai refuses to bow to him, Haman's response escalates beyond personal offense to a plan for the extermination of the entire Jewish population. The extent of this evil reveals the spirit driving Haman. His irritation is not simply emotional; it is fueled by deep-seated hatred and demonic influence. This exemplifies how the enemy operates, concealing his hatred of God's people behind offense, pride, and protocol.

Identifying the real enemy is crucial in spiritual warfare. Esther and Mordecai do not confront Haman directly. Their approach is spiritual: they engage in fasting, prayer, divine timing, and seek God's favor. Their battle is not against flesh and blood but against principalities and powers in heavenly realms.[21]

Haman's scheme to annihilate the Jews was calculated. He persuaded King Xerxes through subtle manipulation, portraying the Jews as a threat to the kingdom's unity. He even offered financial resources to support the genocide. The indifferent king granted Haman his signet ring—signifying unrestrained authority. The decree was sealed, and a date was set for the extermination of God's people.

Yet, God had already orchestrated deliverance while the enemy plotted destruction. Esther was positioned, and Mordecai was attentive. The hidden conflict was unfolding alongside heaven's strategy. The enemy believed he had the upper hand, but God had already placed His people where they needed to be.

This reflects the nature of spiritual warfare. It rarely announces itself with alarms; rather, it hides within systems, decrees, language, and personalities, weaving into culture, policy, and influence. Haman did not arrive with an army; he came armed with a document. The enemy often manifests not through violence but through legislation, persuasion, and access to power.

---

21 Eph. 6:12

We observe this pattern in our modern world. The enemy does not always reveal himself through overt evil; he often disguises himself within narratives, agendas, and ideologies that seem innocuous but harbor destructive seeds. Engaging in spiritual warfare today necessitates discernment that penetrates beyond the surface.

Esther's story equips us to understand that warfare is not always aggressive; it can also be subtle. Haman's ability to convince the king without substantial evidence illustrates how easily deception can infiltrate when discernment is absent. This is why rest is vital in warfare; it quiets our spirits, allowing us to hear God clearly.

Had Esther reacted impulsively, she might have succumbed to panic. Instead, she responded with spiritual wisdom. The distinction is significant: reaction is immediate but often hasty, while response is prayerful, tactical, and grounded. Esther chose to respond thoughtfully.

The hidden conflict encompasses not just external plots but also internal posture. Upon learning of Haman's decree, Mordecai does not rush to the palace in a frenzy. He dons sackcloth and ashes, mourns, and positions himself at the king's gate. This represents a posture of intercession rather than rebellion.

Spiritual warriors recognize the power of lament. Before taking action, there is mourning. Before confrontation, there is consecration. Mordecai exemplifies this beautifully; his grief signifies the weight of the situation.

Haman's plot also illustrates that satanic agendas often intensify when covenant people refuse to bow. Mordecai's simple act of standing became a catalyst for genocide. The enemy is incensed by unwavering faith. He does not require outright denunciation of God; he merely desires submission to pride, fear, culture, and convenience. When one refuses, the agenda is exposed.

However, exposure marks the beginning of strategy. Once Haman's decree is made public, Mordecai communicates with Esther. This is where the battle begins to shift. The quiet queen, hidden within the royal courts, now receives her divine summons. Her moment of rest transitions into a moment of responsibility.

Yet Esther does not act immediately. She sends a message back to Mordecai, outlining the risks. Approaching the king without a summons could lead to death. This is not hesitation; it is wisdom. She comprehends the stakes involved.

Mordecai's response is pointed yet Spirit-led: "Do not think that because you are in the king's house, you alone of all the Jews will escape. For if you remain silent at this time, relief and deliverance for the Jews will arise from another place... And who knows but that you have come to your royal position for such a time as this?"[22]

These words penetrate Esther's fear, reminding her of the divine purpose behind her elevation. She has been chosen not for mere survival but for confrontation, not for silence but for thoughtful action.

From this moment, the narrative pivots. Esther embraces her role in the conflict, yet she does not rush. She calls for a fast, gathers spiritual strength, and aligns her soul. She reminds us that warfare often resembles alignment, consecration, and fasting rather than open conflict.

Haman's introduction in this chapter reveals the nature of the war. Esther teaches us that evil does not always manifest with a terrifying visage. Sometimes, it presents itself in the guise of prestige, power, and eloquence. Therefore, spiritual discernment is essential. Haman's access to the king serves as a caution for all believers: not every open door is divinely ordained, and not every voice in authority speaks for heaven.

Esther and Mordecai do not confront Haman through protest or retaliation. They engage with spiritual posture, employing the weapons of fasting, favor, and wisdom. This serves as our model.

In every generation, Haman emerges, but so does Esther. In every season, the enemy crafts decrees, but so does God. Those who find rest in His presence, discern His timing, and act in accordance with His Spirit will dismantle what hell has orchestrated.

---

22 Est. 4:13-14

Thus, this hidden war is not to be feared but perceived. When you recognize it, you can stand firm. When you stand firm, you can speak into it. And when you speak into it, God moves through you.

From this point forward, Esther transforms from a figure of quiet favor into a weapon of divine warfare. Her presence in the palace was never solely about safety; it was always about strategy.

The unfolding conflict will not resemble traditional battle; it will manifest as fasting, invitation, and divine timing. In all of this, God will be actively moving, though often unseen, for this is how heaven secures victory.

We now transition into one of the most crucial principles in spiritual warfare: warfare often begins in the invisible realm. A shift must occur in prayer before any tangible change takes place in policy or practice. Esther's journey teaches us to look beyond the superficial and recognize where the true battle originates.

Warfare Often Begins in the Invisible Realm

Every spiritual victory is first won in the unseen realm. What we see in the physical world has its roots in the invisible. When Haman issued a decree to destroy the Jews, the public saw a royal order, but those with discernment saw a spiritual attack. It wasn't just a political plot, but a prophetic confrontation between darkness and covenant.

This is why Esther's response wasn't political, but spiritual. She didn't gather an army; she called for a fast. Her response teaches us that spiritual wars aren't fought with worldly weapons, but through obedience, discernment, and spiritual alignment.

The invisible realm is more real than most people understand. It governs outcomes, shapes destinies, and resists purposes aligned with heaven. What Esther faced wasn't just the rage of an offended nobleman, but the eruption of ancient hatred against God's people. To respond effectively, she had to war in the spirit before acting in the natural.

This is a critical truth for modern believers: not all problems can be solved with logic, not all threats are visible, and not all crises begin with what we see. Many battles in boardrooms, homes, churches, and nations began long before a single decision was made. They originated in the spiritual realm.

When Paul wrote in Ephesians 6:12 that we wrestle not against flesh and blood, he wasn't being poetic; he was being precise. The real opposition comes from principalities, powers, rulers of darkness, and spiritual forces of evil. These unseen agents of warfare move through systems, structures, ideologies, and individuals who are unaware they are being used.

Esther and Mordecai modeled how to respond. Their first move wasn't confrontation, but consecration. Mordecai put on sackcloth and ashes, and Esther called a fast. These actions weren't symbolic; they were tactical. They opened access to God's strategy by disrupting the normal pattern of human response.

Fasting is an act of alignment. It silences the flesh so the spirit can hear clearly. It creates space for divine downloads. It disrupts demonic patterns. When Esther called the nation to fast, she declared that the true war was spiritual. The battlefield wasn't in Susa's palace; it was in the unseen.

The people fasted for three days. During that time, nothing publicly changed. The king was unaware. Haman was still plotting. The decree still stood. But in the spirit, the ground was moving. The invisible realm shifts when you fast, pray, and align with heaven. God positions angels. He reveals assignments. He blocks demonic plans.

The key to understanding invisible warfare is recognizing that timing is everything. Esther didn't move during the fast. She waited until the three days were complete. That wasn't hesitation; it was prophetic obedience. Every act in the natural had to match what was unfolding in the spirit.

Rest in warfare comes from this understanding. You don't panic when you trust God is working behind the scenes. You don't react when you know the real conflict isn't with people but with powers. You don't force outcomes when you are aligned with divine timing.

Esther's stillness during those three days was warfare. Her silence was not inactivity; it was surrender. Her confidence came from the fast. She was not going in alone; she was going in under divine covering.

Spiritual warfare in the invisible realm requires insight, not impulse. You must ask God to show you what is really happening. What is behind the attack? What is the root of this resistance? Who is influencing the influencers? The Holy Spirit reveals what flesh cannot see.

Discernment is the skill to see beyond the surface. It is not suspicion or judgment; it is spiritual sagacity that comes through intimacy with God. Esther did not act until she had clarity. And once she did, every move she made was precise, calculated, and Spirit-led.

She was not intimidated by Haman's influence because she understood her authority. Authority is not based on titles; it is based on alignment. Esther's authority came from being in the will of God. When you are aligned with heaven, you carry more weight in the invisible realm than any title can offer.

That is why Haman's plot ultimately failed. Esther moved from rest. She operated in the unseen first. She engaged with heaven before engaging with man. When she approached the king, the spiritual atmosphere had already been prepared.

Every significant breakthrough in Scripture begins with invisible warfare. Moses lifted his hands while Joshua fought in the valley. Daniel prayed for 21 days while angels warred over Persia. Jesus spent 40 days fasting before beginning His ministry. The pattern is consistent.

If you want to see transformation in your situation, you must first ask: what is happening in the spirit? Before reacting to people, inquire of the Lord. Before making decisions, pause for spiritual clarity. Don't be deceived by appearances.

Many believers try to fight spiritual battles with natural tools. They argue, complain, manipulate, or panic. But Esther teaches us a better way: fast, pray, align, and wait for the word. Then act.

The invisible realm also involves angelic movement. Though Esther doesn't mention angels, we know from Scripture that angels respond to the prayers of the righteous. When you fast and pray, you authorize heaven to act. The delay in response is not denial; it is often a battle in the spirit. This is why the three-day fast was necessary. Esther and her people were aligning with God's will, clearing the spiritual atmosphere, and setting the stage.

Haman's spirit still moves today. It works through pride, hatred, and counterfeit authority. It seeks to intimidate, manipulate, and eliminate. But it is no match for a praying church. When God's people rise in discernment and intercession, Haman falls.

Warfare in the invisible realm is also about stewardship. What are you allowing into your thoughts? What words are you speaking? What are you tolerating in your environment? Every choice either strengthens or weakens your spiritual posture.

Esther refused to be reactive. She submitted herself to the process, governed her emotions, waited for peace, and acted boldly, born of prayer.

Invisible warfare also requires community. Esther didn't fast alone; she asked others to join her. There is power in corporate intercession. Jesus said, "Where two or three gather, He is present." Agreement multiplies spiritual effectiveness.

In your own life, who can you fast with? Who can you pray with? Who will stand in the gap with you when the battle intensifies?

This chapter of Esther teaches us to elevate our warfare. Don't just react in the natural. Engage in the spirit. Before confronting the issue, confront the spirit behind the issue. Before stepping into the room, step into the presence of God.

Every breakthrough you seek is already accomplished in the spirit. Your role is to align with it, respond from rest, and act when prompted.

Invisible warfare is not glamorous. It is often lonely. It is misunderstood. But it is powerful. And it is the birthplace of divine reversals.

Esther's decision to fast turned the tide of a nation. Her unseen war birthed visible victory. Her private surrender released public justice. And so it is with you. When you embrace the unseen realm as your true battleground, you stop wasting energy on surface problems. You start engaging heaven. And heaven always wins.

In the next phase of Esther's journey, we will observe how her rest empowers her to respond effectively. When she finally steps into the king's court, she maintains her composure. She chooses to respond rather than react, as true rest in spiritual warfare is about thoughtful responses instead of impulsive reactions.

Rest Means Responding, Not Reacting

Stillness in the spirit is precision and discernment wrapped in peace. In times of spiritual warfare, the distinction between a reaction and a response is crucial in determining whether heaven intervenes or chaos escalates. Esther exemplifies this distinction with remarkable clarity. Her ascent to power and her handling of crisis reveal the strength found in spiritual rest.

When Mordecai first informed Esther of Haman's genocidal decree, she did not react impulsively. Instead, she took her time, asked questions, requested fasting, and awaited guidance and alignment. When the moment arrived, she approached the king not out of desperation but with divine resolve.

This embodies the posture of spiritual authority. Rest does not equate to detachment; it signifies dependence. It allows you to pause, breathe, and refocus on God rather than fear. Reacting means yielding to emotional urgency, while responding means dedication to the authority of heaven.

The difference between reacting and responding extends beyond mere words. Reactions are instinctual and often fueled by fear, anger, or insecurity. Responses are intentional, grounded in prayer, wisdom, and spiritual clarity. Esther demonstrated this after three days of fasting when she entered the king's court. She did not rush in demanding; she simply stood.

That stillness was a wisely farsighted act. The courage required to enter the throne room stemmed not just from personal bravery but from spiritual obedience. She stood at rest, having aligned her soul with God, wrestled with her fear, and entrusted her outcome to the Lord. What followed was a holy response.

When King Xerxes extended the golden scepter, it was not merely a gesture of favor; it signified the unlocking of heaven's strategy. Yet, Esther did not hastily voice her request or mention Haman. Instead, she invited the king to a banquet. This exemplifies the wisdom of spiritual response: it waits for the right timing. Many would have rushed to act, but Esther recognized that the moment was not the end but the beginning of a process. Her rest empowered her to move thoughtfully rather than impulsively.

In challenging times, rest allows you to perceive what others may overlook. It slows your internal pace, enabling you to detect divine signals and avoid engaging in battles that are not yours. Esther did not confront the king out of fear; she created a context where influence could be exercised more effectively.

She organized a banquet, followed by another. She stewarded the atmosphere and positioned the king's heart. This was not manipulation; it was spiritual choreography. Through fasting and prayer, her soul quieted, allowing her to sense the ebb and flow of divine timing.

Responding also necessitates restraint. Esther chose to wait until the second banquet to disclose Haman's plot. This restraint was not a sign of weakness; it was spiritual strength. She understood that revealing the truth too early could be ineffective, while truth shared at the right time holds the power to penetrate.

God had placed Esther, prepared through silence and positioned through favor, and now she was proceeding with peace. Every action she took was a response to the Spirit, exemplifying spiritual maturity.

The enemy seeks reactions, which lead to confusion, chaos, and collateral damage. Reactions are driven by the flesh, inflaming rather than illuminating. In contrast, responses cut through the noise, revealing hidden agendas and releasing divine justice.

Rest protects you from retaliating in your own strength. It grounds you in trust, enabling you to remain calm amid crisis, knowing that God is orchestrating the outcome. When you are secure, there is no need to prove your identity through reaction; you respond from a place of revelation.

Consider how Jesus responded under pressure. He did not lash out at Judas, defend Himself before Pilate, or remain silent in the face of false accusations. Why? Because He was aligned with heaven's plan. His rest facilitated His restraint.

Esther followed this same pattern. She placed her trust in God over her own words, and her response stemmed from intercession rather than impulse.

Believers must learn to lead from this posture. In our homes, workplaces, and ministries, we constantly encounter situations that require a response. The key question is: Are we reacting or responding?

When someone offends you, do you immediately defend yourself? Or do you seek God's perspective first?

When pressure mounts, do you act to alleviate your anxiety? Or do you pursue clarity from the Holy Spirit?

When faced with injustice, do you rush in with your own strategy? Or do you pause, pray, and await divine guidance?

Rest is a strategic approach to warfare. It prevents the enemy from dictating the tempo and allows God to set the pace. It safeguards you from missteps and empowers you to act when the moment is most critical.

Esther did not respond just once; she maintained that posture throughout the process. Even when Haman was exposed, she remained composed, trusting that God would fulfill His plans.

Cultivating this kind of rest requires practice. It does not come naturally. You must learn to embrace silence before speaking, solitude before strategizing, and surrender before taking action.

It also demands confidence in God's justice. You need not engage in every battle when you trust in His faithfulness. You can wait, yield, and move forward with peace.

Responding instead of reacting transforms the atmosphere. It invites heaven into the situation and diffuses negative agendas. Esther altered the tone of the palace not through shouting but by arriving with spiritual clarity.

This clarity is accessible to you, but it must be nurtured. Choose peace over panic, prioritize prayer over opinion, and listen more than you speak. When the time comes to speak, you will do so with purpose. Your words will carry weight, becoming arrows in the hand of the Spirit.

Esther illustrates that the most powerful acts of warfare are often cloaked in rest. Her requests were made gently, yet they carried the force of heaven. She demonstrated that when your heart is still, your voice becomes unstoppable.

Train your spirit to respond. Practice stillness. Incorporate margin into your days. Seek God's help in identifying your triggers. Invite Him to distinguish between holy urgency and human impulse. When you rest in the Spirit, your instincts are refined. Your reactions are transformed. Your decisions align with God's will.

Esther's journey teaches us not to dominate but to discern, to remain anchored when others are anxious, to respond while others react, and to trust when the outcomes are uncertain.

Her posture in warfare was not one of noise, but of presence. And in her presence, change began to occur.

Haman began to unravel. The king began to awaken. The people began to hope. It all began because a woman chose to respond rather than react.

As we continue to explore Esther's story, we will witness the power of calm courage. The tables are about to turn, not through force, but through quiet intervention, faithful presence, and rest that has become a revelation. In this reversal, we learn that discernment always prevails over panic.

Responding with Wisdom in a Rushed World – Esther's Way

In the chaos of my inbox last Tuesday, a single email stood out like a flashing red light: an urgent request from my boss to address a client's complaint. The client, a major account, was threatening to pull their contract over a misunderstanding. My instinct was to fire off a defensive response, to justify our team's actions and prove my competence. My fingers hovered over the keyboard, adrenaline surging. But then, I remembered Esther.

Esther, the queen who didn't rise through force but through faithful response. Esther didn't confront her enemy with noise but disarmed him with discernment. Her story, tucked in the pages of Scripture, felt like a lifeline in that moment. I closed my laptop, took a deep breath, and chose to pause. That pause, I've learned, is the first step to navigating a world that screams urgency but rarely rewards haste.

The Power of the Pause

Esther's life teaches us that every hasty decision carries risk. When Mordecai urged her to approach the king, she didn't rush into the throne room. She paused, seeking divine guidance through fasting and prayer. That pause wasn't indecision; it was wisdom. In my own life, I've started practicing this pause—before replying to a heated text, before saying yes to a new commitment, before spiraling over bad news. Just five seconds of silence, a whispered prayer: "God, what do You see that I don't?" That brief space shifts my heart from reaction to response, from chaos to clarity.

Last week, that pause saved me from an impulsive email. Instead of defending myself, I prayed, waited, and then crafted a response that acknowledged the client's frustration and offered a solution. The client not only stayed but thanked me for my thoughtfulness. Esther's pause had become my strategy.

Prayer as the Foundation

Esther's mission began in private, with three days of fasting and prayer. She didn't act until she'd sought God's perspective. I've started carving out five minutes each morning for silence before God, asking, "What's Your heart for today?" It's not long, but it's enough to anchor me. Before a tough meeting or a family argument, I pray for discernment. This habit keeps me calm, helping me see what's really at stake instead of being swept away by emotion.

Resisting the Tyranny of Urgency

Our world worships urgency. Deadlines, notifications, and crises demand immediate action, but Esther shows us that urgency isn't always from God. She waited for the second banquet, for the king's heart to soften, for divine peace to guide her. When I feel pressured to decide quickly—whether it's a job offer or a conflict—I now ask myself: *Is this pressure holy or manipulative? Am I acting from fear or faith?* Last month, a colleague pushed me to approve a risky project. Instead of caving, I waited, prayed, and realized the proposal wasn't aligned with our goals. Saying no felt like freedom.

Cultivating Discernment

Esther's timing was impeccable because she cultivated discernment. She knew when to speak and when to stay silent. I've started building rhythms to sharpen my own discernment: 30 minutes of solitude each week, journaling what Scripture reveals, and reflecting monthly on moments I reacted instead of responded. One reflection showed me how often I snap at my kids when I'm stressed. Now, I'm learning to pause and ask, "What's this really about?" before disciplining them. The result? Less yelling, more connection.

Rooted in Identity, Not Insecurity

Insecurity makes us react—to defend, to prove, to act when we should wait. Esther, secure in her God-given identity, moved at a measured pace. I've started affirming truths to myself: *I don't need to defend what God has affirmed. I don't need to rush into battles He hasn't assigned.* When a coworker questioned my work last week, I felt the urge to over-explain. Instead, I smiled, nodded, and addressed only what was necessary. My confidence didn't come from their approval but from knowing God had placed me there.

The Art of Asking Questions

Esther didn't assume; she asked. She sought clarity before acting. In every decision now, I try to ask: *What's the real issue here? What outcome is God inviting? Who should I consult?* When my sister and I disagreed about holiday plans, I paused to ask what was driving her frustration. That question led to a heart-to-heart about her stress, not the plans themselves. Our conversation ended in laughter, not conflict.

Strategic Silence

Esther's silence at the first banquet wasn't weakness; it was strategy. She waited for the right moment to reveal her request. I'm learning that silence can speak louder than words. In a recent team meeting, I resisted filling an awkward pause with chatter. My silence let others process, and the discussion deepened. Words spoken at the wrong time weaken; words timed with wisdom wound the enemy and win favor.

Pure Motives, Clear Voice

Before confronting Haman, Esther purified her motives through prayer. She sought God's justice, not personal vindication. Before any confrontation, I now reflect: *Am I honoring God or soothing my pain?* A recent argument with a friend revealed my tone was sharp because of old hurts. I prayed, "Holy Spirit, purify my motives," and apologized. Our friendship grew stronger because my words came from peace, not resentment.

Anchored in Peace

Peace isn't the absence of problems but the presence of God. Esther faced death with calm because she trusted God's sovereignty. I've started grounding myself with Scriptures like Psalm 23 and breath prayers: "Prince of Peace, guide my words." When a project deadline loomed, I repeated, "God goes before me." That peace kept me focused and productive, even under pressure.

The Subtlety of the Spirit

Esther didn't need spectacle; she hosted a banquet. The Spirit moves in subtle ways—a kind word, a timely question, a gentle tone. Last week, a coworker was upset about a missed promotion. Instead of offering advice, I asked, "How can I support you?" That small gesture opened a meaningful conversation. The Spirit is in the subtleties, and I'm learning to trust them.

A Call to Action

Esther's story isn't just history; it's a blueprint. This week, I'm choosing one situation that triggers my impulse to react—maybe a tense email or a family spat. I'll pause, pray, and wait for peace before acting. I'll journal the outcome and share it with a mentor. Already, I've seen how this approach transforms moments of chaos into opportunities for grace.

Reflection and Practice

I'm asking myself: *Where am I reacting instead of responding? What triggers my need to control? Where is God asking me to slow down?* To build responsive strength, I'm committing to weekly listening prayer, memorizing Proverbs 15:1 ("A gentle answer turns away wrath"), and checking in with a friend monthly to reflect on my actions. I'm declaring over myself: *I walk in heaven's wisdom. I respond with clarity, courage, and composure.*

Esther transformed her people's fate not by reacting in fear but by responding in faith. Her stillness was her strength, her silence her strategy. In a world that demands urgency, her story reminds me that I don't need to do everything, just the next right thing. When I move in rest, aligned with God's timing, my steps carry the weight of divine authority. And that's a legacy worth living.

CHAPTER 5

FASTING FOR FAVOR

Is this not the fast that I have chosen: to lose the bonds of wickedness, to undo the heavy burdens, to let the oppressed go free, and that you break every yoke?

ISAIAH 58:6

Esther Calls a Fast—Stillness Before Boldness

Before entering the throne room, Esther embraced stillness. In a moment crucial for her life and her nation, she chose not to reach for a sword or a political ally. Instead, she called upon her people to fast. The strategy from heaven would not arise from haste or human effort; it would be birthed in spiritual alignment.

This moment is significant. With a genocidal decree in place, Haman at the pinnacle of government, and an entire race facing annihilation, Esther's first action was to seek stillness. Fasting became her chosen weapon, showcasing the power of restraint over impulsive reaction.

In Esther 4:15–16, we find her words: "Go, gather together all the Jews who are in Susa, and fast for me. Do not eat or drink for three days, night or day. My attendants and I will fast as you do. I will go to the king when this is done, even though it is against the law. *And if I perish, I perish.*"

These verses are foundational. They mark the transition from a passive beauty queen to an intentional intercessor. Esther could have acted impulsively, reacted in fear, or spoken too soon. Instead, she chose sacred stillness.

This discipline is revolutionary in a world that often prioritizes action. Fasting represents a form of divine resistance. It involves saying no to the immediate to say yes to the eternal. It quiets the body to allow the spirit to communicate. It slows you down so heaven can advance its strategy.

Esther recognized that the power to approach the king could not originate from her strength. It had to come from a source beyond intellect, status, and even natural preparation—from heaven.

She also understood the importance of community alignment. She did not fast in isolation; she invited her people into a unified state of stillness. Collective willingness carries significant weight. When individuals fast together, the spirit of breakthroughs is amplified.

Observe the order of her statement: first fasting, then approaching, then acting. In God's kingdom, boldness emerges from stillness, not haste. Courage is not generated through excitement but cultivated through sacred quiet.

Esther exemplifies the principle that true preparation is spiritual. Prior to the bold action, there is a sacred consecration. Before a strategy is revealed, the soul must be calmed. This is not procrastination; it is empowerment.

Esther understood the gravity of the situation. She did not fast due to a lack of clarity; she fasted because she was about to carry divine authority into the throne room, fully aware of its significance. The fast was not about changing God's mind but aligning her own.

In the life of a believer, fasting transcends mere abstention from food. It signifies a realignment of priorities, focus, and reliance. It is not a performance or a manipulation; it is a surrender. Stillness before boldness prepares your spirit to receive guidance you might otherwise overlook. Esther was not asking God for more courage; she was creating space for clarity.

God often communicates most clearly in silence. Fasting is a deliberate act of quieting the soul, withdrawing from distractions, and adopting a posture of expectation. Esther recognized the necessity of being centered in heaven before confronting adversity.

Her example dismantles the misconception that boldness is synonymous with bravado. It demonstrates that true strength lies not in volume but in vision. She emerged from fasting not with a new speech but with a renewed spirit. She approached the king adorned not only in royal attire but also in spiritual authority.

The fast transformed her. Previously hesitant, she had sent messengers and delayed action. However, after three days of silence, a shift occurred. She did not emerge from the fast awaiting further instructions; she came out ready.

This is a crucial aspect of fasting: it fosters readiness—not in a hurried manner, but in a righteous way. You become alert, attuned, and anchored. Fear of man diminishes because you have been in the presence of God.

Stillness in fasting also reveals what may have been concealed. It purifies intentions, detoxifies pride, uncovers hidden fears, and exposes false strength. It recalibrates your understanding of your identity and purpose.

Esther emerged from the fast with the understanding that favor is not earned but bestowed. She recognized that even if favor did not come from the king, she still had favor with God. This is why she could declare, "If I perish, I perish." It was not a statement of despair but of holy determination.

Fasting shifted her perspective. It enabled her to approach danger with dignity. It allowed her to view her royal position not as a privilege to be safeguarded but as a purpose to be fulfilled.

She no longer acted out of fear of loss; she moved from a place of complete trust. This kind of boldness is not fabricated; it is imparted. It arises from submission, not striving.

When you fast, you align your will with God's timing. You tune your soul to the sound of His voice. You allow the Holy Spirit to excavate, clarify, and sanctify your purpose.

The outcome is unmistakable: you navigate situations with greater peace, clarity, and precision. You carry favor not because you demanded it, but because you embraced stillness.

Esther's choice to initiate a fast illustrates her understanding of kingdom protocol. In the natural realm, she could not enter the king's court uninvited. However, in the spiritual realm, she could enter the throne room with confidence. The fast served as her preparation for both.

Every believer must understand this truth. Earthly authority may impose gates, guards, and protocols, but heaven responds to hunger. When you fast in faith, you gain spiritual access that no earthly system can deny.

Esther's courage to enter the king's presence was not reckless; it stemmed from revelation. She perceived something in the spirit that empowered her to challenge a system while honoring the king. That is wisdom.

In our lives, we will encounter decisions that demand divine discernment. Opportunities require more than strategy; they require surrender. Fasting positions us to receive what cannot be perceived with natural eyes.

It does not guarantee ease, but it ensures alignment. It does not promise applause, but it grants authority. It may not always lead to the desired outcome, but it will always prepare you for what God has ordained.

Fasting is not about proving to God your seriousness. It is about creating space for Him to reveal what is truly at stake. Esther understood the distinction between acting out of emotion and stepping forward from a place of consecration.

She exemplifies a spiritual rhythm: stillness first, then boldness. This was true for Moses at the burning bush, for Jesus in the wilderness, for the early church in Acts, and it remains true for us today.

When Esther broke the silence of her fast, she did not speak out of panic; she spoke with purpose. Her request was not desperate; it was intentional.

Stillness had shaped her, broken the grip of fear, refined her identity, and clarified her authority. She was now prepared to step into the unknown, confident that she carried God's favor.

Favor is not arbitrary; it is not luck. It rests on those who align with God's heart. Fasting is one of the most powerful means to position oneself for that alignment.

Esther did not fast to gain access to the king; she fasted to prepare her soul for the significance of her mission. In doing so, she activated something far more powerful than royal influence: she activated divine timing.

Fasting quiets the distractions of culture and awakens the whispers of heaven. It draws your spirit into sensitivity. It loosens your hold on outcomes and strengthens your commitment to obedience.

This is the essence of Esther's stillness: she ceased trying to protect herself and began preparing herself. She stopped assessing risk and started listening for revelation.

When she stood before the king, heaven had already gone ahead of her.

As we reflect on the unfolding of her courage, the next truth becomes evident: spiritual rest includes active surrender. Stillness was never intended to be idle; it was meant to prepare us for movement led by the Spirit.

Spiritual Rest Includes Active Surrender

Surrender is not a sign of weakness; rather, it is a demonstration of strength directed towards trust. When Esther called for a fast and opted for stillness instead of frantic action, she was not idle. She was submitting to a power greater than her royal status: the hand of God.

Her rest was not passive; it was purposeful. She was strategically surrendering. In the divine economy, that dedication to God became the foundation for victory.

Esther teaches us that genuine spiritual rest does not equate to inactivity. It involves aligning with divine order, relinquishing your will in favor of God's, and choosing dependence when the urge to control arises. The stillness she exhibited before the king was made possible because she had already surrendered in private.

Active surrender encompasses your thoughts, emotions, posture, and plans. It requires you to let go of not only your fears but also your preferences, strategies, timing, and expected outcomes. In this context, rest is a deliberate choice to forgo self-protection and fully rely on God's sufficiency.

This was the stance Esther adopted. She understood the risks involved. Approaching the king without an invitation was a legal offense punishable by death. Yet, rather than seeking a safer alternative, she embraced God's plans: "If I perish, I perish." These words reflected not despair but a release.

Having done all she could spiritually, she prepared to act physically, adorned not only in royal attire but also in the peace that comes from letting go. Her discipline did not diminish her; it empowered her in the Spirit. This is the paradox of the Kingdom: the more you release, the more you carry.

Believers often grapple with the balance between rest and responsibility, fearing that surrender implies passivity. However, spiritual rest does not exempt you from action; it redefines the motivation and posture behind your actions.

Esther still entered the court, made her requests, and hosted banquets, but her actions were rooted in following God, not striving. She did not manipulate the king or attempt to engineer favor; she acted with open hands.

Active surrender involves trusting God's plan and timing, praying without immediate answers, and accepting a lack of clarity. This challenging spiritual practice requires shifting from control to following God's lead.

This posture made Esther effective. She approached the king not in desperation but with dignity, having already surrendered the outcome. When your heart is dedicated to God, your words convey peace—your tone shifts, your motives purify, and your actions become acts of worship.

Esther reminds us that surrender occurs in layers. It begins in the soul and unfolds in steps. First, she listened to Mordecai's guidance. Then, she surrendered to the process of fasting. Next, she yielded to the Spirit's timing. Finally, she surrendered to the risk of action.

Each layer unlocked deeper favor and positioned her for greater authority, achieved without force. Her rest was more powerful than panic, and her stillness accomplished more than shouting ever could.

Spiritual rest combined with active trust in God's plan requires a faith that relinquishes entitlement. Esther did not assume her position would guarantee success. She viewed the crown not as a shield but as a responsibility. Her confidence lay not in her beauty, influence, or timing but in God's faithfulness.

Many struggle at this point. We believe in God, yet cling to our desired outcomes. We fast but demand results. We obey but negotiate timing. Esther surrendered all of this. She did not attempt to control what only God could command. In doing so, she exemplified true spiritual maturity. Maturity is not measured by titles or gifts but by the ability to rest and obey unconditionally. Esther obeyed because it was right, not because it was easy. She rested because God was trustworthy, not because the circumstances were secure.

This kind of surrender fosters intimacy. Esther did not shy away from the crisis; she leaned into it with the Father. Her prayers were not transactional but relational. In that intimacy, she found strength.

Rest without surrender is fragile and breaks under pressure. However, rest coupled with surrender is resilient and can withstand storms. Esther remained calm amid chaos, not due to inside information but because of her deep intimacy with God.

What does this look like in practice?

- It involves pausing before reacting to conflict.
- It means asking, "Lord, what are You doing in this situation?"
- It entails releasing self-imposed timelines.
- It requires choosing integrity over expediency.
- It involves trusting that obedience is never wasted.

Esther let go of her preferences and embraced God's purpose, becoming a vessel for national salvation. Her surrender became a divine conduit.

Surrender is not a weakness; it is a thoughtful act of warfare. It disarms pride, silences striving, and attracts favor.

Esther's story also illustrates that following God often precedes revelation. She did not see the entire picture until she acted. She was unsure of the king's response and lacked assurance of deliverance. Yet, her eyes opened to God's affirmation.

When she entered the court, the king extended his scepter. That gesture was the first visible result of her invisible surrender. Her risk was covered by grace, and her obedience garnered favor. This is how spiritual authority is manifested: not through control but through consecration.

You may find yourself in a place of uncertainty. The stakes may be high, and the outcomes unclear. But if your heart is dedicated to God, you are not unprepared; you are exactly where God wants you to be.

God is not seeking perfect plans; He is looking for surrendered individuals—those willing to exchange their preferences for His purposes, those who will approach thrones and threats with nothing but obedience.

Esther serves as a reflection for every believer called to lead during challenging times. She did not need more skills; she needed more willingness to listen to God. When she offered that, God provided everything else.

Rest is the environment; surrender is the seed. Together, they cultivate boldness.

This is not merely about spiritual posture; it is about spiritual effectiveness. Esther achieved in three quiet days of fasting what an army could not accomplish in years. That is the power of strategic surrender.

Consider these questions:

- Where am I striving instead of surrendering?
- What have I not released that God is asking for?
- Am I at rest in my current struggle, or am I wrestling for control?

The outcome of surrender is supernatural peace. Esther entered danger without fear. She moved lightly because she bore no burdens. Though her hands were empty, her spirit was whole.

You can experience the same. It begins with the courage to let go. Place your rights, fears, timelines, and strategies at His feet, and wait. Allow surrender to work in you.

Esther's story reminds us that Heaven achieves more with a surrendered heart than Earth does with a brilliant mind. Infused with spiritual rest, trusting God opens the next layer of divine guidance: the ability to discern God's strategy in real-time. Esther transitioned into timing, invitation, and intercession, all because she chose to rest, making following God's plan possible.

We are ready to explore how fasting aligns us with God's strategy. Esther did not fast merely to appear holy; she fasted to listen, and what she heard changed history.

Fasting Aligns Us to God's Strategy

When Esther declared a fast, she was not merely abstaining from food; she was positioning herself to receive divine guidance. Her choice to forgo physical nourishment was not about self-discipline but about aligning her thoughts with God's purpose. She understood that the complexity of her mission required clarity that only comes through consecration. Fasting became the pathway to revelation.

God's strategies often diverge from human logic. What seems logical to us may be entirely different from His intended outcomes. This is why fasting is essential during times of decision, danger, or transition. It quiets competing voices and allows heaven's agenda to emerge. For Esther, fasting didn't change God's intentions; it transformed her heart. It silenced the noise of fear and heightened her sensitivity to timing, tone, and tactics.

Fasting serves as a spiritual recalibration. It is the intentional act of saying, "God, I want to hear Your voice—not just what I prefer, fear, or assume." It elevates you from mere reaction to thoughtful response. Esther recognized that without divine guidance, boldness alone would not suffice.

Through fasting, she tuned her ear to heaven. What followed was not random action but tactical brilliance. She did not enter the king's chamber without spiritual awareness; she approached with a clear understanding of her purpose. The fast prepared her to discern what actions to take, how to take them, and when to act.

After the fast, Esther invited the king and Haman to a banquet. This was not merely a social invitation; it was a carefully planned move. The Spirit of God had provided her with guidance for the atmosphere, personalities, and timing. This wisdom was not the result of a committee; it stemmed from her consecration.

The success of her plan lay not in its force but in its timing. The first banquet was not the appropriate moment to confront Haman. She waited, sensing that the king's heart needed further preparation. Such discernment does not arise from impulse; it flows from fasting.

Esther exemplifies that fasting is not a pause before action; it is the beginning of supernatural instruction. It is the moment when God imparts His insights, ensuring that when you act, you do so with certainty instead of guesswork.

God does not always communicate in dramatic ways during a fast. Sometimes the instructions are simple: Wait. Speak softly. Invite again. Refrain from responding. Ask one more question. Yet, these seemingly small nudges can become the blueprint for breakthroughs.

Fasting fine-tunes your spirit to detect frequencies from heaven that the flesh cannot perceive. It enhances your awareness of patterns, undercurrents, and divine opportunities. Esther was not just listening to people; she was attuned to the invisible.

This sensitivity granted her mastery over the situation. Although she lacked political power, she possessed spiritual authority. Her alignment provided her with the power to influence the one who held the signet ring. Haman had earthly influence, while Esther had a heavenly strategy.

Many believers make decisions without seeking God's guidance. They rely on logic, leadership trends, or emotions. However, Kingdom assignments necessitate Kingdom instructions. What was effective in one season may not be applicable in another. This is why alignment is crucial.

Fasting enables you to move from survival mode to tactical clarity. You cease to react to circumstances and begin to discern divine patterns. This shift is vital in spiritual warfare.

Esther's fast unlocked three significant strategic insights:

1. **Discernment of Timing:** She understood not to speak at the first banquet. The Holy Spirit restrained her words to allow the king's heart to soften and Haman's pride to swell. It was at the peak of divine preparation that she ultimately revealed Haman. Such precision only comes when fasting has cleared your spirit of pressure and distractions.
2. **Revelation of Assignment:** The fast clarified that her role was not merely to advocate but to intercede and execute. She transitioned from being a passive observer to a key strategic voice. Fasting reminded her that her elevation was for intercession.
3. **Strategy for Execution:** Her approach to the king, choice of language, sequence of banquets, and revelation of Haman were all orchestrated through spiritual insight. This was not manipulation; it was a revelation.

These discernments were not granted to her because of her title; they were bestowed upon her because she fasted. Titles do not equate to clarity; alignment does.

Believers today must reclaim the practice of fasting as a means of sagacious alignment. It is not a religious ritual; it is a relational repositioning. When you fast, you transition from assumption to accuracy, from desperation to direction, from noise to knowledge.

Fasting not only prepares you for action; it also prepares your environment. While Esther fasted, the spiritual climate around her shifted. The king's sleep was disturbed, and Mordecai's loyalty was remembered. The groundwork for reversal was laid while she remained still.

This is the outcome of fasting in faith. God moves behind the scenes, preparing hearts, unraveling plots, exposing motives, and highlighting overlooked details. While you silence your flesh, heaven amplifies its voice on earth.

Fasting is the gateway to supernatural momentum. It generates ideas you could not have conceived independently. It creates space for strategies that transcend natural laws. It equips you with wisdom for timing, speech, and action.

Esther did not need to shout, campaign, or plead. She simply responded to what God had revealed to her. That is spiritual alignment. When you fast, your focus shifts from being seen to remaining sensitive.

In a fast-paced world that values urgency, fasting teaches you the importance of waiting. In that waiting, you receive strategies that are not just clever; they are sovereign. Alignment is about posture. Fasting repositions you, humbles you, and makes you aware that success is not about being right; it's about being in rhythm with heaven.

Esther's rhythm was cultivated through silence. Her movements were deliberate, and her impact was significant. But it all began with consecration.

Fasting brings convergence. Heaven's plan and your obedience intersect, leading to a breakthrough.

Consider these questions:

- Have I taken the time to truly hear what God is saying?
- Am I assuming that my willingness equates to readiness?
- Do I need to fast to recalibrate my timing, tone, or tactics?

God continues to reveal strategies to those who seek Him in stillness. He guides His people through spiritual insight rather than surface-level responses.

Esther's fast marked a turning point—not because she compelled God, but because she opened her heart. In that openness, God provided a strategy that dismantled an empire's evil agenda.

You have access to that same insight, but it will not be found in haste. It will be discovered in humility.

As the next chapter unfolds, we see Esther take the strategy she received and implement it with boldness and grace. What fasting unlocks, obedience releases. Now, we step into the moment where preparation meets power, as Esther, guided by divine strategy, makes her decisive move.

Fasting for Clarity: A Modern Reflection on Esther's Approach

In a world that demands constant motion—emails piling up, decisions looming, and notifications buzzing—stillness feels like rebellion. Yet, it's in this deliberate pause that we find clarity, the kind that Esther discovered when she faced a crisis that could have ended her life and her people's future. Her story, tucked in the pages of the Old Testament, isn't just a historical account; it's a blueprint for navigating pressure with purpose. Esther's fast was not a performance or a ritual to check off. It was a public declaration of trust, a quiet act of surrender that unlocked divine strategy. Her example challenges us to rethink fasting—not as a religious chore but as a practical tool to realign our hearts, sharpen our decisions, and invite God's favor into our lives.

I learned this the hard way last spring, staring down a career decision that felt like a tightrope walk. Should I take the promotion, uproot my family, and move across the country? Or stay in the familiar, even if it meant stagnation? The noise was deafening—colleagues' advice, my own doubts, and the endless pros-and-cons lists. I needed clarity, not just more information. That's when Esther's story found me, not through a sermon but through a quiet nudge to try something radical: fasting. Not to twist God's arm for an answer, but to listen.

Day One: Silence and Surrender

On the first day of my three-day fast, inspired by Esther's example, I chose water only—no food, no coffee, no scrolling through my phone. I started with Esther 4, where she calls her community to fast with her, facing a life-or-death moment. Her fast wasn't about proving her devotion; it was about quieting the chaos to hear God's voice. I prayed, "Lord, calm my spirit so I can hear You." Sitting in my living room, phone silenced, I journaled my deepest fears: *What if I make the wrong choice? What if I fail?* The act of writing them down felt like handing them over. Fasting wasn't just about skipping meals; it was about creating space for God to speak.

Esther's fast teaches us to listen, not compete. She didn't fast to outdo anyone or earn divine favor. She fasted to align her heart with God's. Before big decisions, we must ask: *What voices am I hearing? Do I need more data, or deeper intimacy with God? Is my next step driven by fear or clarity?* Fasting strips away distractions, filters emotional noise, and anchors us in trust. For me, that first day revealed how much I'd been leaning on my own logic instead of divine guidance.

Day Two: Clarity and Cleansing

By day two, hunger was real, but so was a growing sense of focus. I read Psalm 51, a cry for a clean heart, and John 10, where Jesus speaks of knowing His voice. My prayer shifted: "Lord, refine my motives and open my ears." Fasting wasn't just deprivation; it was a cleansing process. I noticed how my need for control surfaced—my fear of uncertainty, my tendency to overplan. Journaling helped me name what I needed to release: *I'm trying to control the outcome instead of trusting You.* Esther's fast was purposeful, aimed at protecting her people but also positioning her for God's strategy. I defined my own focus: clarity about the job decision and peace regardless of the outcome. Writing it down made it real, inviting divine instruction.

Fasting requires intention. Esther's three-day total fast matched the urgency of her crisis, but not every fast needs to be so intense. A partial fast, like eating only vegetables, or a soul fast, like cutting out social media, can be just as powerful if done with purpose. The key is to choose a sacrifice that challenges you and a stillness that transforms you. That day, I turned off notifications and let worship music fill my apartment. The quiet wasn't empty; it was alive with possibility.

Day Three: Strategy and Strength

By the third day, I felt lighter—not just physically, but spiritually. Reading Esther 5, I saw how she moved with precision after her fast, speaking with wisdom and timing that saved her people. I also read 2 Chronicles 20, where Jehoshaphat's fast led to a divine battle plan. My prayer became, "Lord, grant me discernment for timing and communication." In the stillness, a subtle strategy emerged: not a booming revelation, but a clear sense that the promotion wasn't my path. I journaled action steps: *Decline the offer. Stay where I am. Trust God for the next opportunity.* The peace that followed wasn't tied to the outcome; it was rooted in surrender.

Esther didn't fast alone; she invited her community to join her. I'd asked two close friends to pray with me, and we shared insights over text. Their perspectives amplified my own, reminding me that collective fasting builds spiritual momentum. After the fast, I didn't retreat into comfort. I acted on the clarity I'd received, emailing my boss to decline the promotion with gratitude and confidence. The result? A new project opened up locally, one that aligned with my skills and values in ways I couldn't have planned.

Lessons from Esther's Fast

Esther's fast wasn't about guaranteeing safety; it was about preparing her heart. She surrendered before she strategized and trusted before she triumphed. Her story offers practical steps for us today:

- **Define your purpose.** Write down what you're seeking—clarity, breakthrough, or guidance. Specificity sharpens your focus.
- **Choose your fast intentionally.** Match the intensity to your need, whether it's a full fast, partial fast, or soul fast.
- **Center on worship and the Word.** Start with Scripture, pray intentionally, and journal what you sense. God speaks in the quiet.
- **Invite allies.** Ask trusted friends to join you in prayer or fasting. Unity strengthens discernment.
- **Embrace silence.** Dedicate time to stillness daily. Let God's whispers shape your strategy.
- **Surrender, don't manipulate.** Fast to align with God, not to control outcomes. Pray, "Transform me before my circumstances."
- **Notice what emerges.** Fasting reveals fears and motives. Don't suppress them; bring them to God.
- **Record insights.** Document Scriptures, promptings, and patterns. Strategy comes through small revelations.
- **Act on momentum.** After the fast, take immediate steps based on what you've heard. Faith requires action.

Reflection and Action

As I reflect on my fast, I ask myself: *Have I used fasting to manipulate God or to align with Him? What's stopped me from fasting regularly? Where do I need clarity that I haven't fasted for?* These questions, inspired by Esther, push me to approach fasting with anticipation, not obligation. Her fast reminds us that spiritual warfare often begins quietly, in hunger and surrender. It's not about loud demands but about saying, "God, guide me before I act."

This week, I'm planning another fast—a soul fast from media to focus on a family decision. I've invited a friend to join me, and I'm setting aside 30 minutes daily for silence. My journal is ready to capture what God reveals. Esther's fast wasn't a one-time event; it was a rhythm that fueled her boldness and grace. Her story invites us to do the same: to fast with purpose, listen with expectation, and act with faith. When we do, we don't just change our circumstances—we change ourselves.

Call to Action

Plan a fast this week. Choose a focus, invite a friend, and eliminate distractions. Journal daily, and act on what you hear. As Esther shows us, clarity follows consecration, and favor follows surrender.

CHAPTER 6

Bold Moves, Soft Steps

Have I not commanded you? Be strong and of good courage; do not be afraid nor be dismayed, for the Lord your God is with you wherever you go.

Joshua 1:9

Esther Approaches the King With Grace, Not Force

The scripture notes, "On the third day Esther put on her royal robes and stood in the inner court of the palace, in front of the king's hall."[23] This single moment carries more significance than many battles.

Esther did not demand an audience or force her way in. Instead, she stood with a posture of following God, relying on her humility rather than her status as queen. This act touched the heart of the king. When the king saw her, he extended the golden scepter. Although the law could have condemned her, her fasting signaled her hope for life. It was her posture, not her protests, that created access; her presence, rather than her petitions, that opened the door.

23 Est. 5:1

This moment illustrates a profound truth in spiritual leadership: grace achieves what force cannot. Esther approached the highest earthly authority with the calmness of one who had already submitted to the highest authority in heaven.

This is the essence of boldness in the kingdom. It does not roar; it walks. It does not impose; it invites. It does not manipulate; it ministers.

Esther was bold yet gentle. Her approach was confident but not confrontational. Her words were respectful, not demanding. She understood timing, tone, and tact, which made her words resonate far beyond their volume.

Often, boldness is confused with brashness. Yet Esther redefines courage. She did not allow fear to silence her, but she also did not let enthusiasm overshadow wisdom. She was precise, measured, and intentional.

She recognized that the outcome belonged to God; her role was to be obedient.

Spiritual maturity discerns when to speak, how to stand, and what to say. Esther waited for the fast to conclude before donning her royal robes. This was not vanity, but strategy. She honored the environment she was entering, aware that her appearance carried significance. She approached the moment with intention.

This exemplifies spiritual grace. It is not passive; it is purposeful. It allows one to enter tense situations without adding to the tension, to bring peace into chaos, and to change the atmosphere through presence rather than pressure.

Esther did not need a crowd or a loud voice. She required clarity, favor, and courage—all of which she found in God's presence.

Her bold move was not merely entering the court; it was waiting for the right moment. She could have spoken immediately, but instead, she invited the king to a banquet. And then another.

This is the benefit of fasting. It provides the patience to wait and the discernment to understand why. Had she spoken too soon, the plan might have failed. Grace granted her restraint. The Holy Spirit was orchestrating every detail, and Esther chose not to rush.

Her restraint was not hesitation; it was respect. She honored the king's heart, God's timing, and the process. In doing so, she safeguarded the strategy God had given her. Spiritual boldness requires courage and self-control.

Esther's steps were soft, yet her spirit was strong. She did not retreat; she submitted her boldness to grace. The result? The king offered her anything she desired—up to half the kingdom.

This offer stemmed not from a demand but from discernment. When grace leads, favor follows.

Esther teaches us that many significant victories begin with presence. Before she spoke, she stood. Before she asked, she waited. Her posture set the tone, and her peace elicited a response.

When she finally spoke, it was not to expose but to invite. "If it pleases the king," she said, "let the king and Haman come today to a banquet I have prepared for him."

She invited her adversary to the table, not to flatter but to frame the situation. She was setting the stage, aligning with heaven's plan.

Spiritual leaders today must learn from Esther. Boldness is not recklessness; it is grounded in revelation. And revelation does not shout; it illuminates.

Her invitation to Haman was not a compromise; it was clarity. She recognized who he was, but she also understood her own identity. And she was unafraid.

Boldness rooted in grace is not intimidated by darkness. It is purposeful in its confrontation. Esther did not expose Haman publicly—not yet. She allowed the tension to build, giving pride the chance to overreach. That was wisdom, not weakness.

At the first banquet, she still refrained from speaking. Once again, she invited the king and Haman to another banquet. She was pacing the moment, not delaying out of fear but discerning in faith.

Every soft step was intentional. Every pause was meaningful. In between banquets, God was at work. The king could not sleep. Mordecai's honor was recalled. The atmosphere was shifting.

That is what grace accomplishes. It trusts that God is moving even while you are waiting.

Esther's approach reveals that sometimes warfare manifests as a whisper, as waiting, as walking slowly through volatile situations. Boldness does not need to crash through doors. It can stand in the hallway, enveloped in peace, knowing that heaven is opening the way.

There is no need to rush. What is needed is to listen. There is no need to dominate. What is required is discernment.

Esther's grace established a rhythm of response. Every moment was governed by restraint. Every word was guided by wisdom. Every action was supported by heaven.

The second banquet arrived. This time, the trap was set. And Esther, still speaking with grace, revealed the truth. She exposed Haman not with venom but with clarity. She spoke not as a victim but as a vessel.

Her words were straightforward. Her request was simple: "Spare my life and the lives of my people." And truth, delivered with grace, dismantled evil.

The king was furious. Haman was undone. The shift in power had begun.

None of this required Esther to change who she was. She did not adopt aggression. She did not abandon honor. She remained true to who God had created her to be: bold, strategic, and surrendered.

Your most significant victories will emerge from grace—the kind that moves slowly, listens intently, and acts only when heaven says, "Now."

Let Esther be your guide:

- Soft steps are not weak.
- Silence can be a strength.
- Presence shifts atmospheres.
- Timing is crucial.
- Boldness is not about noise; it is about vision.
- And the most powerful vision is always born in the secret place.

What Esther demonstrates next is that her grace-filled boldness not only wins favor but also dismantles the enemy's plans. Her spiritual posture becomes the gateway through which God's justice flows. Because what you move into with soft steps, God finishes with a mighty.

Strategic Intercession as Warfare

When Esther exposed Haman's plot, she unmasked him. Her intervention didn't involve accusation; it brought illumination. She created an atmosphere where truth had no choice but to surface. And that's one of the most extraordinary acts of war.

True intercession uncovers injustice without shouting, reveals darkness without hysteria, and moves in the grace of revelation, not the aggression of reaction.

Esther's tactical intercession began long before she spoke up. It started with her fasting, deepened in her waiting, matured at the banquet table, and culminated in a moment that seemed simple but held the power of heaven: a spoken truth at the right time, in the right setting, with the right spirit.

This isn't the kind of warfare that breaks doors. This is the kind that bends kingdoms.

When Esther interceded for her people, she wasn't pleading from weakness. She was declaring from alignment. She had fasted, listened, and waited. She had crafted a moment under heaven's guidance.

Strategic intercession always precedes significant shifts. Esther she moved with her prayer, acted on her revelation, and stewarded intercession all the way through execution. Many fail to follow that model. We often stop our intercession at the prayer altar. But Esther carried it into action. She partnered with God both in private and also in public. She understood that intercession leads to intervention.

Esther didn't just save her people through favor. She saved them through warfare rooted in mercy and built on truth.

Her decision to speak was the product of divine design. The banquet table was a battleground. Her request was a sword. Her tone was a shield. And the Spirit of God fought through her composure.

Strategic intercession requires two core spiritual muscles: sensitivity and stamina. Sensitivity allows you to discern when, where, and how to pray. Not every burden is meant to be blurted. Some are meant to be carried. Some are meant to be prayed through in phases. Esther's fast sharpened her sensitivity.

Stamina keeps you consistent even when you don't see immediate results. Esther hosted one banquet, then another. She remained in position, unmoved by delay. Every great intercessor understands that heaven's timelines differ from earth's. But if you stay aligned, the breakthrough will come.

Esther's voice carried power because it came from posture, not panic. She had waited with the Lord. And when she finally spoke, her voice was amplified by all the silence that preceded it.

Her intercession wasn't begging. It was a confident petition based on covenant. She knew the Jewish people were chosen. She knew God had made promises. She stepped into her moment, knowing she was standing in agreement with heaven.

Esther didn't approach the king asking him to imagine the evil that was coming. She presented the reality. She called it what it was. That bold clarity was the fruit of spiritual accuracy.

Strategic intercession is warfare because it challenges the unseen.

- It challenges principalities.
- It confronts hidden agendas.
- It confronts timelines meant to destroy.
- It disrupts demonic momentum.

And it does all of that with elegance. Esther shows us that you don't have to shout to shift a nation. You only need to speak when heaven says, "Now."

Esther's appeal to the king was clear: "If I have found favor in your sight… spare my life and the lives of my people." In that single sentence, she moved her case from personal to national. From isolated to corporate. She merged her identity with theirs. She interceded not as royalty but as a daughter of the covenant. That is the highest form of intercession: to lay down your personal image for the sake of collective destiny.

The warfare of intercession also includes precision. Esther didn't accuse without proof. She laid the situation before the king in a way that required action. She didn't make it about herself. She made it about justice. And justice demands a response.

Intercession doesn't just ask God to move—it invites people to move too. The king had to respond. The courtroom shifted because the atmosphere had been prepared in the prayer room.

Intercessors must understand this: prayer is preparation. But what you do after prayer matters just as much. Are you willing to speak? To risk? To move?

Esther did all three.

Her intercession also gave God legal access into the realm of Persian governance. She had been positioned in the palace for a purpose. She used her access not for self-promotion, but for intercession.

God places people in positions of influence for this reason. To intercede with wisdom. To expose without rage. To speak without flattery. Esther did all of this—and it turned the heart of a king.

Your authority in the spirit is not based on volume. It is based on vision. Esther had vision. She saw the strategy. She walked it out. And her intercession dismantled the most well-funded genocide plan of her era. All without raising her voice.

You may be in a political, hostile, or spiritually dry place right now. But if God has positioned you, you are equipped for thoughtful intercession. You are not there by chance. You are a key.

Pray while others panic.

Speak while others speculate.

Host while others hurry.

Wait while others war.

Because tactical intercession flips the script. It reveals what's hidden. It softens what's hardened. It ignites what's dormant. It reverses what's irreversible.

Esther was not just a queen. She was a spiritual weapon. And her intercession didn't just delay destruction. It birthed deliverance.

As we step into the next revelation in her life, we will watch how the rhythm of boldness and rest continues to unfold. Esther's next moves will show us that grace and guidance walk hand in hand, and that God does far more in stillness than we ever could in striving.

Timing and Wisdom Are Key—God Does More in Stillness Than We Can in Striving

God is never late. And He is never early. He moves in exactness. This divine precision is difficult for a generation conditioned to hurry, but it is the very rhythm of the Spirit. Esther walked in this rhythm with remarkable clarity. Her story is not just one of bravery—it is a masterclass in timing and wisdom. And her restraint teaches us that heaven's strategy does not bow to earth's pressure.

When Esther entered the king's inner court, her decision had been marinated in three days of fasting. That fast didn't just prepare her courage—it tuned her discernment. She didn't rush to deliver her request. She waited. She didn't speak at the first opportunity. She paused. That pause wasn't fear; it was Spirit-led foresight.

She knew that if she moved too soon, she could derail the deliverance God had orchestrated. Boldness without timing is recklessness. But boldness coupled with wisdom becomes prophetic execution.

Timing and wisdom are inseparable when it comes to spiritual impact. Timing speaks to the "when." Wisdom speaks to the "how." Esther operated in both. She walked into the moment already synchronized with heaven.

At the first banquet, she had the king's full attention. His affection was stirred. His favor was overflowing. Yet she withheld her request. This is the mark of maturity. When you can speak—but choose to wait.

Too many people lose the battle in the moment of almost. They jump at the opportunity instead of discerning if it is the right one. Esther saw the opening but recognized it was not the appointed time. Her spirit told her: wait again.

Waiting is warfare. And waiting is wisdom. Because every time you wait in surrender to God, heaven is arranging something you cannot see. Between Esther's first and second banquet, the king lost sleep. That wasn't a coincidence—it was divine orchestration.

The king's insomnia led him to discover Mordecai's act of loyalty. That honor had been overlooked—until now. At the very moment Esther was pausing, God was preparing. That's what He always does. In your waiting, He is working.

This is the power of stillness. When you stop striving, you give space for God to move. Stillness is not inactivity. It is spiritual cooperation. Esther cooperated with God by not rushing. And that cooperation triggered a chain of heavenly events.

While she waited, the king read the chronicles. He remembered Mordecai. He asked, "What has been done for this man?" Nothing had been done. And in the divine irony of heaven, Haman walked in at that moment—ready to suggest Mordecai's death, but instead, commissioned to honor him. Timing isn't luck. It is the product of surrender to God.

Esther didn't know the king couldn't sleep. She didn't know what Haman was planning. But she didn't need to. She trusted that heaven was engineering what her wisdom could not see.

When the second banquet arrived, Esther knew the time had come. There was a spiritual shift. She had waited. She had obeyed. And now, she could move.

Her words were clear. Her tone, composed. Her heart, anchored.

"If I have found favor with the king," she began, "and if it pleases Your Majesty, grant me my life—this is my petition. And spare my people—this is my request."

She didn't accuse. She didn't expose too early. She presented the truth with grace and let the weight of it settle into the room.

Wisdom is not just about knowing what to say. It's about knowing when to say it. Esther said it at the right time, in the right tone, to the right audience. And that moment broke everything open.

The king was enraged. Haman was terrified. The hidden plot came to light. And the pivot of history began. If Esther had spoken too soon, it would not have carried the same weight. Her discernment allowed God's justice to be timed perfectly.

God does more in stillness than we can in striving. This is why learning to wait is so vital. Waiting is not wasted time. It is preparatory time. It is when God sets the table while we wait at the door.

Esther's wisdom wasn't loud. It was low, quiet, humble. It flowed from fasting, not from force. Wisdom is not knowing all the answers. It is knowing what not to say. It is knowing when to pause. It is trusting that heaven's calendar holds your breakthrough.

Every believer is called to walk like Esther. To resist the urge to rush. To be bold—but not brash. To be ready—but not reactive. You will find yourself in rooms of opportunity. You will feel the impulse to speak. But ask: is it time? Is this the word? Is this the audience?

Timing sanctifies the bold word. Wisdom shields the obedient act. Together, they release power.

The reason Esther's request carried authority was because it had been seasoned in silence. It had been bathed in prayer. It had been timed by heaven.

Esther's life is a reminder that rushing is not boldness. And silence is not weakness. Some of your most potent spiritual moves will be preceded by long pauses. Holy hesitations. Divine delays.

Don't panic in the pause.

Learn to listen longer. Wait for the nudge. Follow peace, not pressure.

If God says speak—speak. But if He says wait—wait. Even if it looks like the moment is slipping away. Even if others don't understand. Even if your own emotions scream, "Now!"

The king's sleepless night came because Esther waited. Mordecai's public honor came because Esther paused. Haman's exposure came because Esther trusted.

Nothing you give to God is ever lost. Every pause in obedience is packed with purpose. He is always doing more in the stillness than you think. What feels like delay is divine orchestration. What feels like silence is spiritual strategy. What feels like inactivity is preparation for impact.

Let Esther's timing encourage you:

- It's okay to wait twice before speaking once.
- It's okay to appear slow if God is doing something deep.
- It's okay to let your wisdom outpace your words.

Because when the moment comes, the words you've waited to say will carry more than opinion. They'll carry authority. And that authority not only turns the head of a king, but also turns the tide of history.

As we now move deeper into the unfolding of this divine turnaround, the story of Esther reveals how the subtle strength of spiritual wisdom prepares the way for justice. Her ability to wait was not her weakness—it was her weapon. And the justice that follows will not be rooted in vengeance. It will be rooted in rest.

Because the tables are about to turn. And when they do, the glory will belong to the One who moves in stillness more powerfully than we ever could through striving.

Spiritual Boldness in Action: Maya's Story

In the sleek, glass-walled office of a bustling tech startup, Maya sat at her desk, her laptop screen glowing with an email that could change everything. The subject line read: *Urgent: Project Proposal Approval Needed*. Her team had been tasked with pitching a bold new initiative to the company's board—a project that could redefine their market presence but carried significant risks. As the youngest project lead, Maya felt the weight of expectation pressing against her chest. Her instinct was to fire off a response, to assert her vision with force and urgency. But something deeper stirred within her, a quiet nudge to pause. She remembered the story of Esther, a queen who embodied boldness not through loud demands but through gentle steps, a surrendered spirit, and purposeful actions.

Maya leaned back in her chair, closed her eyes, and took a deep breath. *Slow down to hear clearly*, she thought, recalling how Esther's greatest strength was her ability to listen to God before acting. Esther didn't rush into the king's court with a rehearsed speech; she waited, prayed, and fasted, letting divine clarity shape her strategy. Maya whispered a quick prayer: "Holy Spirit, what do You want to reveal to me here?" She resisted the urge to assume she had all the answers, choosing instead to wait for a sense of peace. In the silence, she felt a prompting to review the proposal one more time, to ensure it aligned with the company's mission and her team's values. That pause, she later realized, saved her from presenting a plan driven by ambition rather than purpose.

As she prepared for the board meeting, Maya reflected on what was driving her boldness. Was it her calling to lead this project, or was it a need to prove herself? Esther's bravery came from a deep sense of identity and mission—she acted for her people, not her ego. Maya journaled her thoughts, asking herself: *Is this about control or calling? Am I defending my pride or following the Spirit's guidance?* She remembered Esther's three days of fasting, a deliberate act to purify her motives. Maya decided to fast from social media for a day, clearing her mind of external validation and focusing on the project's true purpose: to serve the company's clients and her team.

Timing, Maya realized, was as critical as intention. Esther didn't speak at her first banquet with the king; she waited, trusting God's pace. Maya had been tempted to push the proposal through quickly, fearing the board might lose interest. But she recalled Esther's restraint and asked herself: *Am I doing this because I can or because I must?* She sought counsel from a mentor, who advised her to wait for the board's quarterly review, when they'd be more receptive. Maya also meditated on Ecclesiastes 3:7—"a time to be silent and a time to speak." Trusting that delays might be divine protection, she chose to refine the proposal further, ensuring every detail was ready when the moment arrived.

When the day of the presentation came, Maya thought about how Esther packaged bold truth in grace. Esther didn't accuse Haman outright; she revealed the truth with a tender tone that disarmed the king. Maya knew the board might resist her proposal's ambitious scope, so she approached the meeting with humility. Instead of demanding approval, she asked questions: "How can we ensure this aligns with our long-term vision?" Her tone was confident yet respectful, inviting collaboration rather than confrontation. To her surprise, the board responded with enthusiasm, appreciating her thoughtfulness. *Your tone often influences whether your truth is accepted*, she noted, grateful for Esther's example.

Maya also considered her environment carefully, just as Esther chose a banquet over a courtroom to share her message. The boardroom was formal, but Maya requested a smaller, informal pre-meeting with key stakeholders to gauge their receptiveness. This allowed her to share insights in a setting where hearts were open, avoiding the risk of miscommunication in a high-pressure context. *The right message in the wrong context can lead to confusion*, she reminded herself, choosing her moments of vulnerability with care.

Dressing for the moment was another lesson from Esther, who wore royal attire to reflect her authority and honor. Maya prepared her spirit through prayer and worship the morning of the meeting, centering herself in God's presence. Practically, she chose a professional yet approachable outfit, signaling her readiness without seeking attention. *How you present what God has entrusted to you reflects your stewardship*, she thought, ensuring her appearance aligned with her assignment.

Throughout the process, Maya protected her strategy in silence, just as Esther kept her plans private until the right moment. She documented her ideas in a private journal, sharing them only with her mentor and a trusted colleague. *Wisdom protects what passion might hastily disclose*, she reflected, praying daily for guidance on when to act. This discipline kept her focused and prevented premature exposure that could have derailed her efforts.

Maya's identity as a woman of faith shaped every decision. Like Esther, who didn't hide her heritage when the time came, Maya brought her values into the boardroom. She spoke confidently about the project's ethical implications, ensuring it served not just the company but the community. *Boldness is not just about what you say; it's about who you remain*, she reminded herself, refusing to fragment her faith to fit in.

When the board finally approved the proposal, Maya knew it was because she had prepared during the stillness. Like Esther, who acted decisively when God said "now," Maya had practiced obedience in small matters—revising drafts, seeking feedback, and affirming daily, "Yes, Lord—whatever You ask." Her readiness allowed her to step forward with courage when the moment arrived.

Reflecting on the experience, Maya asked herself the questions Esther's story inspired: *Where am I speaking too soon? What is God asking me to wait for? Who should I approach with grace instead of force?* She committed to a weekly silence practice, spending 30 minutes with her phone off, listening to God. She also chose one difficult conversation each month to approach with kindness, meditating on Proverbs 25:11: "A word fitly spoken is like apples of gold in a setting of silver." Her declarations became a daily anchor: *I operate in God's timing, not man's. My tone conveys truth enveloped in grace. I am led, not hurried.*

Maya's journey mirrored Esther's in its quiet courage. By pausing, listening, and moving with purpose, she saw God's justice unfold—not through striving or shouting, but through alignment with divine whispers. The project's success was more than a professional win; it was a testament to the power of spiritual boldness, proving that gentle steps and a surrendered spirit can dismantle obstacles and open doors.

Call to Action

Identify one situation where you're pushing instead of pausing. Commit to 24 hours of silence on that issue, listening and inviting God to speak. After the pause, document what wisdom reveals, and act only when peace, timing, and tone align. Like Esther, let your boldness be rooted in rest, and watch how stillness achieves what force cannot.

CHAPTER 7

The Tables Turned

When the Lord brought back the captivity of Zion,
we were like those who dream.

Psalm 126:1

Haman's Downfall and the Divine Reversal

Haman reached the height of his power, driven by pride and a deep-seated animosity towards Mordecai. His intentions extended beyond punishing one individual; he aimed to annihilate an entire nation. The 75-foot gallows he constructed stood as a stark representation of his desire to obliterate God's people. However, in a dramatic turn of events, those same gallows became the instrument of his own demise.

As the Scriptures recount, while Haman basked in his influence, believing himself invincible, a series of divine occurrences took place. The king's sleepless night, a seemingly minor detail, became a pivotal moment in history. God, who remained unseen and unnamed throughout the book of Esther, orchestrated events with remarkable precision. The king, restless and seeking solace, requested the book of records to be read, rediscovering Mordecai's overlooked act of loyalty that had saved his life.

Timing and providence converged. Just as Haman entered the palace to advocate for Mordecai's execution, the king was contemplating how to honor Mordecai. The irony was striking, almost poetic. Haman, who had plotted Mordecai's downfall, found himself leading a public procession in Mordecai's honor, proclaiming, "This is what is done for the man the king delights to honor!"24 Each word must have struck Haman's pride like a dagger.

Yet the ultimate reversal was still to unfold. At Esther's second banquet, her strategy, developed through fasting, prayer, and divine timing, came to fruition. She revealed her true identity as a Jew and exposed Haman's nefarious plot. Her words were few but impactful. The atmosphere shifted. The king's fury erupted. Haman, once untouchable, now pleaded for his life, collapsing upon Esther's couch in utter humiliation. The very gallows he constructed for Mordecai became his own execution site. Divine justice was swift and unmistakable.

This exemplifies God's reversals: thorough, precise, and irrefutable. The story of Esther illustrates that when God acts, He not only delivers His people but also dismantles the forces of evil arrayed against them.

For believers today, Haman's downfall helps us understand that every scheme of the enemy, every plot woven in darkness, is visible to God. The gallows of destruction the enemy erects can become platforms for God's glory. What was intended for shame, God transforms into honor. What was designed to break you, God turns into breakthrough. Haman's downfall illustrates that pride leads to destruction; his schemes were overturned by God's sovereign plan to protect His people.

There is profound encouragement here: divine reversals may not be immediate, but they are assured for those who remain aligned

---

24 Est. 6:11

with God's purposes. Esther and Mordecai's patience, discernment, and trust paved the way for a victory only heaven could orchestrate.

Esther's redemption mirrors Christ's victory, where the cross became a symbol of triumph over death. Satan's plan for destruction was transformed into the means of eternal life. God's fingerprints are always present in the reversal, even when His presence seems concealed.

This chapter in Esther's story signifies a transition—from defense to dominion. What began as a covert struggle culminates in public vindication. As we will see next, Esther and Mordecai step into a new season of authority and decree, shaping the future with wisdom forged in conflict.

For when God turns the tables, He does not merely rescue; He repositions.

God's Justice Flows Through Quiet Courage

God's justice, as illustrated in Esther's narrative, encompasses both the visible and invisible aspects of our reality. While the king's decree and Haman's gallows were evident to all, the spiritual conflict underlying these events remained concealed. Esther's fast engaged with this unseen realm, aligning her people with God's intentions and inviting a divine justice that transcended human limitations.

Haman's downfall represented the dismantling of a malevolent agenda. God eliminated Haman and reversed the entire decree he had initiated. This exemplifies God's justice: it not only halts the enemy but also reverses his actions, restores what was lost, and uplifts the oppressed.

A significant principle emerges here: even seemingly small acts of courage can unleash profound justice in the spiritual realm. Esther's willingness to risk her life before the king effectively thwarted the plans of darkness.

Quiet courage manifests as speaking the truth when it's challenging, fasting when others indulge, and waiting for God's timing when the urge to act prematurely is strong. This courage is powerful. And God's justice is carried forth by it.

Esther's story also highlights the connection between divine justice and identity. She had to publicly embrace her Jewish heritage to fully fulfill her mission. Similarly, your courage is most potent when you are fully aligned with your God-given identity.

Justice in the Kingdom is also restorative. The exposure and execution of Haman did not conclude the story; Mordecai was elevated, and new decrees were enacted to protect the Jews. God's justice punishes the wicked and also uplifts the righteous and secures a future for those who have endured suffering.

Esther's quiet courage inspired others. What began as her personal obedience ignited national repentance, collective fasting, and a unified return to faith. Her stand reminded the people of their covenant identity and drew them back to their God.

In our lives, God's justice is often realized through similar principles. When we choose integrity over compromise, humility over pride, and prayer over panic, we position ourselves as instruments of justice. While it may not occur immediately, justice is inevitable when we adhere to heavenly principles.

Esther's courage dramatically shifted the palace atmosphere. A place that had previously been indifferent to her people became the backdrop for their deliverance, demonstrating how faith can transform policy and culture. This illustrates that in modern contexts like workplaces, communities, or governments, the quiet courage of one person aligned with God can spark justice and righteousness.

Furthermore, Esther's courage safeguarded future generations. The reversal of Haman's decree spared those living at that time and also ensured the continuity of the Jewish lineage through which Christ would eventually come. God's justice, manifested through Esther's bravery, had eternal significance.

We must acknowledge that divine justice does not always unfold at our desired pace. Esther and Mordecai experienced prolonged periods of waiting and uncertainty. However, when the appointed moment arrived, God's justice was swift and thorough. His timing is impeccable, even when it tests our patience. Our role is to maintain our courage, stand in faith, and trust that His justice is already in motion, even if it is not yet visible.

As Esther's story illustrates, no opposition is too entrenched, no scheme too advanced, and no evil too formidable for God's justice to overturn. Quiet courage is the key that unlocks divine intervention.

In the next chapter of Esther's journey, we will witness how the power of stillness—allowing God to fight the battle—brings about extraordinary victory. The justice that begins with quiet courage ultimately leads to undeniable triumph.

The Power of Standing Still and Letting God Fight

When Moses led the Israelites out of Egypt, they found themselves caught between Pharaoh's army and the Red Sea. In that pivotal moment, God's message through Moses was clear: "Don't be afraid. Stand firm and you will see the deliverance the Lord will bring you today."[25] Their victory came not from their own efforts, but from their posture.

Esther's story reflects this same principle. Her willingness to remain steadfast highlighted God's intervention. The salvation of the Jews was not solely credited to her, but to God's unseen hand working through those who were willing to follow His plan.

Maintaining stillness also shields us from the urge to strive. Striving often stems from fear—the belief that if we don't take action, nothing will change. In contrast, stillness arises from trust—the assurance that God is faithful to complete what He begins.

In Esther's situation, once everything was revealed, the king's authority took charge. Haman was removed, and Mordecai was elevated. Esther didn't need to control every outcome. Her bravery opened the door; her stillness allowed God's justice to enter.

In your own life, recognize when to act decisively and when to let God take the lead. Standing still doesn't equate to inaction. It means doing your part and then surrendering the outcome. It

25 Ex. 14:13

involves praying fervently while avoiding panic. It requires thorough preparation coupled with confident rest.

Esther illustrates that after you have done everything—prayed, fasted, planned, and spoken—you can find peace. You can trust that God's justice is at work, even when it's not visible. The results often exceed what you could have orchestrated on your own.

This posture of stillness also nurtures your spirit. It protects you from burnout and bitterness. It liberates you from the illusion of control and reminds you that God is the true architect of victory.

Esther's legacy teaches us that sometimes your most impactful action is to wait. To observe. To allow God to demonstrate His faithfulness.

As we move into the next chapter of her journey, we will witness the fullness of that victory—the divine vindication that only heaven can orchestrate, reminding us that rest and trust are not the conclusion of the battle, but the pathway to overwhelming triumph.

Finding Victory Through Stillness – My Reflection

The email landed in my inbox like a thunderclap: *"Urgent: Budget cuts may impact your department."* My heart raced as I read the words, my mind spiraling into worst-case scenarios. Layoffs? Reduced hours? I wanted to fire off a reply, schedule a meeting, or at least draft a plan to secure my team's future. But something stopped me—a quiet nudge, almost imperceptible, urging me to pause. In that moment, I remembered Esther, a woman whose story taught me that victory often comes not from frantic action but from spiritual alignment, rest, and trust in God's timing.

Esther faced a crisis far greater than mine—a decree threatening her people's annihilation. Yet, she didn't rush into the king's court with demands or panic. Instead, she fasted, prayed, and waited, aligning herself with God's plan. Her story became my guide as I navigated this workplace storm, teaching me to blend courage with stillness, preparation with surrender. Here's how I applied her timeless principles to my challenge, and how you can too.

First, I needed discernment. Esther knew when to act and when to wait, a balance I often struggle with. I started asking God daily, "Is this a time for action or stillness?" Instead of emailing my boss immediately, I journaled my thoughts and sought Scripture for clarity. Psalm 46:10—"Be still, and know that I am God"—became my anchor. Patience wasn't easy, but it allowed me to see the situation evolve, revealing details I would have missed in haste.

Preparation was next. Esther didn't approach the king haphazardly; she strategized, fasted, and prayed. I prepared for a potential meeting with my supervisor, researching budget trends and drafting solutions for our department. But once prepared, I released control. Standing in my kitchen, I whispered, "I've done my part; God, handle Yours." This act of surrender lifted a weight I hadn't realized I was carrying.

Esther's respect for authority also struck me. She honored the king, even while challenging injustice. I chose to approach my boss with humility, framing my concerns as collaborative ideas rather than demands. Before our meeting, I prayed for favor, asking God to soften hearts. To my surprise, my boss listened intently, and the conversation opened doors to creative solutions.

Timing was critical. Esther waited for the right moment to reveal Haman's plot, trusting God's signal. I felt tempted to push for immediate answers, but I sought peace instead. I waited for confirmation—through prayer, a mentor's advice, and a sense of calm—before speaking up. The delay wasn't wasted; it allowed me to present my case when my boss was most receptive.

Releasing control was the hardest step. My instinct was to micromanage every detail, but Esther's example of stillness inspired me. I began praying, "Lord, I release my grip on this outcome." I noticed my anxiety triggers—late-night emails, rumors of layoffs—and countered them with intentional rest, like a quiet evening walk or a moment of worship. These small acts grounded me in trust.

As days passed, I celebrated small shifts. A colleague's encouragement, a budget meeting postponed—these were signs of God's movement. I thanked Him daily, sharing these wins with a trusted friend who prayed with me. Esther's victory wasn't instant, and neither was mine. But each step forward built my faith.

The community was vital. Esther rallied her people to fast and pray, amplifying her victory. I invited two coworkers to join me in weekly prayer, and their support strengthened my resolve. We held each other accountable, checking in on our faith journeys and praying over shared challenges.

When I finally spoke in the meeting, I chose my words carefully, inspired by Esther's concise yet powerful speech. I prayed for wisdom beforehand, aiming for clarity over anxiety. The outcome wasn't perfect, but my willingness opened doors for compromise—a restructured budget that preserved jobs.

The victory brought new responsibilities. Esther and Mordecai didn't rest on their laurels; they led forward. I stayed humble, seeking God's guidance for the next steps and remaining vigilant for new tasks. My department's stability felt like a divine reversal, but I knew the work wasn't over.

Reflecting on this journey, I asked myself: *Where am I called to act boldly? Where must I stand still? What outcome do I need to release?* I invited my prayer group to join me in focused intercession, and we celebrated every small victory. To reinforce this mindset, I adopted daily declarations: "I am bold and discerning. My victory is secured by God's strength." Weekly worship and monthly reflections kept me grounded, while a seasonal fast deepened my trust during this transition.

Key Reminders

If you're facing a challenge, try this: Identify where you're tempted to control the outcome. Commit to three days of prayer and stillness, then document what God reveals. Share your journey with a mentor or prayer partner. Remember, God's justice unfolds perfectly, even in delays. Stillness isn't weakness—it's spiritual warfare. Divine reversals follow divine alignment, and obedience opens doors that striving cannot.

As I await the final outcome of my workplace challenge, I'm reminded of Esther's legacy. Her rest became the foundation for heaven's declaration on earth. By aligning with God's plan, I'm learning to trust that victory is already in motion—whether I see it yet or not.

CHAPTER 8

The Decree of Dominion

You will also declare a thing, and it shall be established for you; So light will shine on your way.

Job 22:28

Esther and Mordecai Write a New Decree

Victory in the spirit translates to authority in the natural realm. Esther's journey reached a pivotal moment: the enemy's scheme was uncovered, Haman had been defeated, and Mordecai had been elevated. However, the threat was still present. The decree permitting the destruction of the Jews was still in effect.

Esther and Mordecai stepped into this moment with courage. Their focus shifted from personal survival to national transformation. The king entrusted Mordecai with his signet ring, a powerful symbol of delegated authority. With this power, Esther and Mordecai drafted a new decree, overturning the original death sentence. The Jews were empowered to defend themselves, gain strength, and achieve victory over their oppressors.

This serves as an important lesson for believers: victory isn't complete until new decrees are made. Remaining silent after deliverance allows old patterns to resurface. Esther and Mordecai recognized that spiritual breakthroughs require prophetic declarations. They didn't merely celebrate their enemy's defeat; they established a new reality through the authority they had been granted.

Scripture tells us, "Mordecai wrote in the name of King Xerxes, sealed the dispatches with the king's signet ring, and sent them by mounted couriers, who rode fast horses especially bred for the king."[26] This urgency underscores the seriousness of their mission. They acted swiftly to secure their people's freedom.

Their decree was wisely farsighted. It didn't abolish the previous law (which Persian policy prohibited), but it empowered the Jews with the legal right to defend themselves. This approach ensured that when the day of attack arrived, the Jews were no longer passive victims but active participants in their own deliverance.

This moment resonates with us today. Every spiritual victory must be affirmed with declarations that align with God's promises and establish His authority in our circumstances. It's not sufficient to experience private deliverance; we must publicly declare what God has accomplished and what will now stand as truth.

Esther and Mordecai's decree illustrates the principle of delegated authority. They weren't kings themselves, but they operated with the king's power. As believers, we are seated with Christ in heavenly places, endowed with His authority to declare and implement heaven's will on earth. The signet ring has been placed in our hands through the Holy Spirit.[27]

The urgency and boldness of their decree remind us that the enemy's defeat is only part of the battle. Establishing new dominion completes the process. We cannot leave spiritual voids. Where darkness once prevailed, we must establish the flag of righteousness.

26 Est. 8:10

27 Eph. 2:6

Notice the inclusivity of the decree. It was sent "to the Jews in every province of the empire."[28] No one was excluded. Every community, regardless of how remote, was granted access to the new law. God's justice is comprehensive, and His deliverance extends to everyone willing to receive it.

This teaches us that breakthroughs in our lives are not solely for our benefit. They ripple outward—to our families, communities, workplaces, and cities. When we achieve victory, we are called to issue decrees that invite others into the same freedom.

Esther and Mordecai's courage to draft and release a new decree transformed a moment of survival into a movement of empowerment. Their leadership turned a vulnerable people into a victorious army. This exemplifies the power of prophetic declaration.

As we will see, their decree did not go unnoticed. It sparked action. The Jews rose with renewed confidence, defended their families, and experienced overwhelming victory. None of this would have occurred had Esther and Mordecai remained silent after their initial breakthrough.

Victory demands a voice. Dominion requires a decree.

The Power of Prophetic Declaration and Spiritual Authority

In our lives, prophetic declaration operates similarly. We may encounter medical diagnoses, financial difficulties, relationship issues, or spiritual struggles that feel overwhelming. However, when we declare God's promises with faith and authority, we invoke heaven's counter-decree. The effectiveness lies in the alignment of our spirit.

Esther and Mordecai's strategic decree empowered the Jews. It enabled the people to gather, safeguard their families, and reclaim what had been threatened beyond mere survival.

For us, this means we utilize prophetic declarations not just to maintain our position but to expand our influence. We aim to reclaim

---

28 Est. 8:9

what has been lost and to advance God's Kingdom in every aspect of our lives.

It's crucial to recognize that their decree was issued "in the name of King Xerxes" and sealed with his ring. Authority is significant. Similarly, our spiritual declarations must be grounded in the authority of Jesus Christ. This is not about wishful thinking or mere affirmations; it's about proclaiming God's word with divine endorsement.

The Bible states, "You will also decree a thing, and it will be established for you; and light will shine on your ways."[29] This verse encapsulates the principle embodied by Esther and Mordecai. Their decree sparked national transformation, bringing light where darkness had prevailed.

Another important aspect of their declaration was its extensive reach. The decree was disseminated to every province, city, and corner of the empire. This was intentional; no Jew was to be left uninformed or unprepared. Spiritually, this reminds us to ensure that our declarations encompass all areas of our lives. We cannot afford to leave any territory—spiritual, emotional, relational, or physical—unprotected.

Esther and Mordecai's example illustrates the importance of persistence. They continued to strive for complete breakthrough for their people. Their declarations were not one-time events—they were sustained until realized.

In your journey, persistence is vital. Continue declaring God's promises. Keep aligning your words with His truth. Even when circumstances appear unchanged, trust that heaven is working behind the scenes.

Additionally, Mordecai's decree inspired action. The Jews rose, emboldened by the spoken word. Prophetic declarations should not be passive. They ignite faith, courage, and movement. When you declare God's word, be ready to act on it. Partner with your declarations by stepping out in compliance to God's plan.

---

29 Job 22:28

Ultimately, the story of Esther highlights that prophetic declaration is about covenant partnership. Mordecai and Esther aligned themselves with God's covenant for their people, and their decree emerged from that alignment. The authority of your words is directly linked to the depth of your relationship with God.

As we continue with Esther's story, we will see that rest does not equate to silence. It involves speaking from a place of confidence, authority, and divine partnership—declaring heaven's truth until it becomes reality on earth.

Rest Doesn't Mean Silence—It Means Confident Speech

There is a common misconception in spiritual life that rest equates to inaction or silence. However, Esther's story effectively challenges this idea. While spiritual rest involves submission and trust, it also allows for confident, Spirit-led communication. Rest does not mean a lack of words; rather, it is about speaking words that are aligned with divine purpose.

After fasting, praying, and discerning, Esther's words were bold. They were filled with authority, precision, and grace. This is the balance that believers must learn to achieve: resting in God's sovereignty while speaking with His authority.

Esther's demeanor reflected rest, yet her voice was clear and powerful. When she approached the king, she confidently stated what needed to be said, knowing that the Spirit had prepared both her heart and the king's.

This type of confident communication stems from a close relationship with God. Esther had laid the groundwork through fasting and alignment. Her words were not rushed or reactive; they were delivered at the precise moment of divine opportunity.

For believers, resting without confident speech can lead to complacency, while speaking without rest can result in mere noise. When these two elements come together—being both willing and bold—we express spiritual authority.

Esther's bold speech accomplished what human strategies could not. It garnered royal favor, revealed wrongdoing, and changed her people's fate. Her voice, shaped by respect for God, became a powerful instrument for justice. It is essential to recognize that her speech emerged from a place of peace with a goal to share truth. Confident speech does not manipulate but reveals God's heart.

In your own life, resting in God does not exempt you from speaking. It prepares you to communicate at the right time, with the right words, and in the right manner. Whether advocating for justice, standing for truth, or declaring God's promises, let your words reflect the boldness exemplified by Esther.

Scripture reminds us: "Let the redeemed of the Lord say so."[30] Declaration is part of our spiritual inheritance. We rest in what God has done, while also proclaiming what He is doing and will do.

Confident speech is characterized by:

- Clarity: Understanding exactly what you are asking or declaring.
- Courage: Speaking out even when fear tries to hold you back.
- Conviction: Grounding your words in God's truth, rather than personal opinion.
- Composure: Communicating with peace, not panic.

Esther embodied all of these qualities. She was concise and clear in her message: "Grant me my life—this is my petition. And spare my people—this is my request."[31] Simple. Direct. Unwavering.

For many believers, embracing confident speech involves overcoming the belief that your words lack significance. Proverbs 18:21 states, "Death and life are in the power of the tongue." What you say can influence outcomes. Remaining silent during divine prompting can hinder breakthroughs. Esther's story teaches us when it is time to speak up.

Confident speech also requires discernment. Esther waited for the right moment to speak. She invited the king and Haman to two

30 Ps. 107:2

31 Est. 7:3

banquets before sharing her words. Timing enhanced her impact. This illustrates that not every moment is appropriate for speaking. However, when God prompts you with "Now," hesitation is not humility—it is disobedience. Confident speech responds when the Spirit leads.

Moreover, Esther's words were declarations aligned with God's covenant promises to Israel. Her speech held power because it resonated with God's will. Similarly, your declarations carry authority when they are grounded in Scripture and aligned with heaven's agenda.

Restful boldness also disarms opposition. Haman anticipated silence or submission, but Esther's confident speech dismantled his plans. When you speak from a place of spiritual rest, your words resonate with divine precision.

It is important to establish a routine of declaring truth regularly—not just in times of crisis. Cultivate daily practices of confession and declaration that reinforce God's promises in your life.

- Morning declaration: Begin your day by affirming God's faithfulness and promises.
- Midday reset: During stressful moments, take a pause to speak peace over your mind.
- Evening reflection: Conclude your day by expressing gratitude to God for His guidance and victories.

By doing this, you train your spirit to remain anchored and your words to remain impactful.

Esther's breakthrough teaches us that the combination of rest and confident speech invites extraordinary outcomes. After you have fasted, prayed, and prepared, speak boldly. Trust that God has gone before you, and know that your Spirit-anointed words will achieve more than your efforts ever could.

As we continue through Esther's journey, we will observe how her confident speech set in motion a significant reversal—demonstrating that when we stand in rest and speak with authority, we not only influence moments but also shape history.

Bold Declarations from a Rested Heart – My Reflection

The room was quiet, save for the soft hum of my morning coffee maker and the faint rustle of pages as I opened my Bible. It was 6 a.m., and the world outside was still cloaked in the gentle hush of dawn. This was my time—my sacred pause before the day's demands swept me into their current. I had learned, through trial and error, that these moments of stillness were not just a luxury; they were my lifeline. Like Esther, who fasted and prayed before stepping into the king's presence, I was learning to anchor my words in God's presence before letting them loose into the world.

Esther's story had gripped me lately. Here was a woman who faced a crisis that could have crushed her, yet she moved with a confidence that seemed to flow from a deeper well. Her rest and trust in God's authority weren't passive; they were the foundation of her bold speech, her decrees that shifted the fate of a nation. As I sat with her story, I began to see my own life through its lens. My words, too, could carry weight—if I aligned them with God's plan. But how? The answer, I found, lay in practical, intentional steps that transformed my heart and speech into instruments of divine dominion.

My first step was cultivating a discipline of stillness. Esther didn't rush into the king's court with a hasty petition; she prepared her heart through fasting and prayer. I started setting aside ten minutes each morning to sit in silence, asking God, "What do You want me to say today?" I kept a journal nearby, scribbling down prompts like, "What is God showing me that needs to be spoken?" When a coworker's cutting remark tempted me to fire back, I paused, took a breath, and sought God's counsel first. That pause became my shield, guarding my words from impulsiveness and grounding them in His wisdom.

Next, I began writing personal decrees rooted in Scripture. Esther and Mordecai's decree was precise, backed by the king's authority. I searched the Bible for promises that spoke to my current battles—verses like Isaiah 54:17, "No weapon formed against you shall prosper." I turned these into declarations: "I am protected by God's promises; no attack against me will succeed." Each morning, I spoke them aloud, letting their truth settle into my bones. The act of speaking wasn't just repetition; it was a declaration of alignment with God's Word, a staking of my claim in His kingdom.

Timing, I learned, was as crucial as content. Esther waited for the right moment, even when the first banquet seemed like the perfect opportunity. I started asking God, "Is now the time to speak?" When a family conflict arose, I sought counsel from a trusted mentor, weighing whether my words would build or break. I learned to follow the peace in my spirit as my green light, trusting that God's timing would amplify my words' impact.

Clarity became my ally. Esther's petition was brief but piercing. I practiced stripping my words to their core truth, cutting out fluff that diluted their power. Before a tough conversation with my boss, I rehearsed my points, ensuring they were clear and direct. "Speak with clarity, not complexity," I reminded myself, and the result was a conversation that shifted our dynamic for the better.

My words needed to carry kingdom authority, like Esther's decree sealed with the king's signet ring. I began praying in Jesus' name—not as a ritualistic tagline, but as a conscious acknowledgment of His authority backing my words. I regularly checked my heart, asking, "Do my declarations reflect God's heart?" Empty affirmations had no place; every word I spoke needed to be anchored in Scripture's truth.

Boldness didn't come overnight. Like Esther, whose courage grew from accepting Mordecai's charge to making her ultimate request, I started small. I spoke up in a team meeting, sharing an idea I'd hesitated to voice. Afterward, I reflected: "What did I learn?" Each small act built my confidence, and I celebrated the progress, no matter how small. These moments were training grounds for greater battles.

Esther didn't win alone; she invited her community to fast and pray with her. I formed a small prayer circle with two friends, sharing my declarations and asking for their intercession. When God moved, I shared the testimonies—how a strained relationship healed after a bold conversation, how a financial need was met after I declared His provision. These stories didn't just encourage me; they inspired my friends to step out in faith, too.

Worship became my anchor. Starting my declarations with praise kept my focus on God, not myself. I played worship music as I journaled, letting songs of truth fuel my faith. After every significant conversation, I closed in worship, thanking God for His movement, even when the outcome wasn't yet clear.

Tracking results strengthened my faith. Like Esther and Mordecai, who saw tangible victories, I kept a record of breakthroughs—answered prayers, shifted relationships, opened doors. Each month, I reviewed my journal, noting where God had moved and adjusting my strategies. Sharing these victories publicly, whether in a small group or a quick post on X, gave God glory and encouraged others.

As I reflected, questions stirred: Where had I been silent when God prompted me to speak? What fears held me back? How could I prepare spiritually for bold speech? Who could I partner with in prayer? What Scripture was God highlighting for me to declare? These questions became my roadmap, guiding me toward a lifestyle of rest-fueled dominion.

Practical Steps to Build Bold Dominion

- **Weekly Word Declarations:** Choose one Scripture each week to declare over your life. For example, "I am positioned in Christ's authority."[32]
- **Monthly Boldness Review:** Reflect on moments you spoke boldly or held back. Adjust your approach for the next month.
- **Quarterly Fasting & Alignment:** Set aside a day each quarter to fast, pray, and recalibrate your declarations with God's heart.

---

32 Eph. 2:6

- **Ongoing Prayer Journaling:** Record your declarations and their outcomes to track God's faithfulness.

Declarations to Speak Over Your Life

- I am positioned in Christ's authority.
- My words align with heaven and shift atmospheres.
- I speak with boldness, clarity, and peace.
- God's promises are yes and amen in my life.
- Breakthrough follows my obedience.

CALL TO ACTION

Take one area where you've hesitated to speak boldly. Write a Scripture-based declaration for it, like "I will not fear, for God is with me."[33] Speak it daily for 30 days, invite a friend to pray with you, and document how God moves.

Key Truths to Remember

- Rest is the foundation; speech is the extension.
- You are not speaking alone—heaven backs your words.
- Timing is as crucial as content.
- Every declaration rooted in God's Word is a seed for breakthrough.
- Bold speech from a rested heart transforms not just moments but legacies.

Esther's journey teaches us that victorious Christian living flows from a rested heart aligned with God's authority. When we prepare in stillness, speak with clarity, and move in His timing, our words become seeds of breakthrough, planting legacies that echo beyond our lifetime.

---

33 Isa. 41:10

CHAPTER 9

VICTORY ESTABLISHED

For whatever is born of God overcomes the world. And this is the victory that has overcome the world—our faith.

1 JOHN 5:4

The Jews Defend Themselves and Prevail

The moment of deliverance has finally arrived. The Jewish people, once facing annihilation, now stand empowered. Through the authority conferred by Esther and Mordecai's decree, they transitioned from passive recipients of mercy to active defenders of their own victory.

Scripture states, "On the very day the enemies of the Jews had hoped to overpower them, the tables were turned, and the Jews gained the upper hand over those who hated them."[34] This divine reversal was a testament to God's unwavering faithfulness. United and courageous, the Jews defended themselves, achieving victory over their adversaries throughout Persia.

34 Est. 9:1

The victory was comprehensive. The Jews repelled their attackers, earning the respect and fear of neighboring peoples. The evidence of God's hand was clear. What the enemy intended for harm was transformed into a foundation for strength.

Esther's bravery and Mordecai's wisdom prepared the people for this pivotal moment, but it was the ordinary men and women who stepped forward in faith to fight the battle. This underscores a vital truth: while God's decrees set the stage, our submission to God and actions bring them to fruition. The Jews did not wait passively for victory; they took a stand, fought with conviction, and trusted in God's presence.

The extent of the victory was extraordinary. In Susa alone, 500 men were defeated, including Haman's ten sons, ensuring that his lineage could no longer threaten God's people. Throughout the empire, in every region where the Jews faced danger, they triumphed. The fear of Mordecai, now a significant figure in the king's court, spread widely, and his influence ensured the protection of the Jewish people.

This historic victory serves as a reminder that spiritual warfare transcends personal deliverance. God's justice is thorough. He not only rescues us from peril but also establishes us in strength and authority.

It is noteworthy to mention the restraint shown by the Jews. Despite their victory over their enemies, they refrained from seizing plunder. This self-discipline underscored their alignment with God's purposes and enhanced their honor in the eyes of the Persian people.

For believers today, the victory of Esther's people serves as a model. It illustrates that when God's decrees are proclaimed and His people rise in faith, no opposition can prevail. The challenges you face may seem daunting, but with God's authority supporting you, you are called to thrive.

Victory is achieved when:

- God's promises are boldly proclaimed.
- His people act with faith and courage.
- Obedience is prioritized over comfort.
- Integrity is upheld even in success.

The Jews' victory was a visible manifestation of an invisible battle won. Heaven had intervened, and the earth responded. Their enemies were defeated, but more importantly, a spiritual stronghold was dismantled. Fear, intimidation, and hopelessness gave way to confidence, joy, and renewed faith.

This chapter in Esther's narrative teaches us that true victory is not solely about the conclusion of a battle; it marks the beginning of a new season. For the Jews, this signified the dawn of security and peace. For Esther and Mordecai, it solidified their divinely appointed leadership. And for the Kingdom of God, it stands as a testament that no scheme of the enemy can succeed when God's people remain steadfast in His promises.

As we approach the conclusion of Esther's remarkable story, we will see how this victory was a lasting legacy for generations to come.

The Outcome of War From Rest: Overwhelming Triumph

The remarkable success of the Jewish people illustrates an essential principle: when challenges are approached from a place of rest—trusting and aligning with divine strategy—the results can exceed expectations. Rest involves proactive surrender, allowing individuals to silence fear and panic, enabling them to hear God's guidance, understand His plans, and act with precision.

The story of Esther demonstrates that true victory originates from inner alignment. The Jewish people triumphed because their spirits were in harmony with God's purposes. Their fasting, prayers, and steadfast faith prepared them for a breakthrough that defied natural odds.

Overwhelming triumph in the Kingdom has a dual impact: it delivers God's people and serves as a testament to His greatness. Your personal victories are intended to glorify God and draw others to His power and faithfulness.

The triumph of the Jews also underscores the importance of preparation. While their victory stemmed from rest, they were not passive. The decree allowed them to defend themselves, but they had to act. They united, armed themselves, and stood ready. Rest does not equate to neglect; it means doing everything possible and then trusting God to enhance your efforts.

This principle is applicable today. When facing spiritual battles—whether in personal life, ministry, or leadership—it is crucial to first align with God through prayer, fasting, and dedication. Once aligned, you must step out in faith, prepared and expectant. This partnership between divine sovereignty and human responsibility leads to overwhelming triumph.

Moreover, Esther's story illustrates that victory extends beyond immediate circumstances. The triumph positioned them for influence and longevity. Mordecai's promotion and the Jews' elevated status within the Persian Empire ensured their safety and prosperity for years. This teaches us that God's victories provide relief, restoration, elevation, and expansion. When you engage in battle from a place of rest, you allow God to achieve far beyond what you can ask or imagine.

Another crucial aspect of this triumph was the unity among God's people. The Jews came together to defend themselves, demonstrating that victory in the Kingdom is usually a united effort. The leadership of Esther and Mordecai inspired the people to act in unity, thus creating a force that the enemy could not fathom.

In your own challenges, seek a spiritual community. Surround yourself with those who will pray with you, support you, and proclaim God's promises alongside you. There is significant power in unified faith.

Lastly, overwhelming triumph brings lasting peace. After the battle, the Jews celebrated their deliverance with joy and feasting. They transitioned from mourning to rejoicing, from fear to celebration. God's victories always culminate in joy.

As we move forward in Esther's story, we will see how this overwhelming triumph was not only remembered but institutionalized—how rest, joy, and worship became the ongoing rhythm of a people who witnessed God's mighty hand at work on their behalf.

Learning to Fight From Victory, Not For Victory

One of the most transformative lessons from Esther's story is the transition from striving for victory to operating from a place of victory. Following the new decree, the Jews stood in a position of assured triumph, implementing what had already been established by divine authority.

This shift in mindset is vital for believers today. Too often, we engage in battles as if we are trying to achieve victory, overlooking the fact that in Christ, victory has already been secured. The decree from Esther and Mordecai represented a settled matter; the Jews' responsibility was to enforce what had been decreed, not to create victory from nothing.

This principle resonates throughout Scripture. In the New Testament, Paul reminds us, "But thanks be to God! He gives us the victory through our Lord Jesus Christ."[35] Victory is a gift, not a goal. Our role is to embrace that victory, apply it, and enforce it in every aspect of our lives.

Esther's people exemplify this beautifully. The decree had been issued; their authority was established. Yet, they still needed to take up arms and stand firm. This illustrates that living in victory is not passive; it's an active alignment with heaven's decree. It's not about striving for uncertainty but standing resolutely in what is already established.

This distinction reshapes how we confront challenges. Instead of praying from a place of desperation—"Lord, please grant me victory"—we can declare with confidence: "Lord, I thank You that victory is mine, and I stand in it today."

Operating from victory also transforms your emotional state. Fear, anxiety, and striving give way to peace, assurance, and boldness. Esther and her people approached their battle with calmness, preparedness, and confidence in God's justice. This settled assurance empowered their actions to be both powerful and precise.

---

35 1 Cor. 15:57

To fight from victory, believers must deeply trust God's promises, developed through prayer, fasting (like Esther), and Scripture. It is strengthened by immersing ourselves in Scripture, allowing God's truth to overwrite every lie of the enemy. Victory-based warfare also requires a prophetic perspective. Esther and Mordecai looked beyond the immediate threat to the larger picture. Fighting from victory means viewing your battles in light of God's eternal plan.

Another important aspect is the power of testimony. The Jews' remarkable triumph became a narrative that spread across the empire, reinforcing their identity as God's covenant people. Testimony fortifies your position. Each time you recall and declare what God has already accomplished, you strengthen the victory mindset.

To implement this mindset practically:

- **Start with gratitude:** Thank God daily for victories, both seen and unseen.
- **Declare your position:** Speak aloud, «I am more than a conqueror through Christ.»
- **Reject panic:** When challenges arise, pause and remember that you are enforcing, not earning, victory.
- **Worship as warfare:** Praise God not for what you hope will happen, but for what He has already achieved.

Fighting from victory also means recognizing that battles will still arise. Esther's people were not immune to attack because of the new decree. What changed was their authority and confidence. Similarly, believers will encounter trials, but these trials present opportunities to apply and showcase the victory of Christ.

Esther's reminds us that victory is a mantle we carry with us, not something we chase after. Reflect on whether you strive for victory or operate from it. How would your prayers, declarations, and actions change if you believed that the battle was already won in Christ?

As we approach the concluding chapters of Esther's story, we will witness how this established victory becomes a lasting legacy—a victory remembered, celebrated, and woven into the rhythm of worship and rest for generations to come.

Living in Victory – My Reflection

The story of Esther is not just a historical account of a queen who saved her people; it's a vivid illustration of what it means to live in victory—not as a fleeting moment, but as a way of life. Esther's triumph over Haman's plot wasn't a one-time event. It was the culmination of a mindset rooted in confidence, peace, and trust in God's unshakable decree. Her story teaches us that victory is not something we chase; it's something we stand in, day after day, through intentional habits and a heart aligned with heaven.

I used to think victory was about crossing a finish line—landing the job, overcoming a struggle, or seeing a prayer answered. But Esther's life shows us something different. Victory is a posture, a lifestyle that flows from knowing who God is and what He has already accomplished. It's waking up each morning and choosing to live as if the battle is already won—because, in Christ, it is. Over time, I've learned that embracing this mindset requires practical steps, daily choices, and a willingness to see every moment as an opportunity to enforce heaven's triumph. Here's how I've begun to live this out, and how you can too.

Shifting My Words, Shifting My World

One of the first changes I made was in how I prayed. I used to approach God with a laundry list of requests, pleading for help as if victory was uncertain. "God, please help me get through this," I'd say, my voice tinged with doubt. But Esther didn't beg; she stood firm in God's promise. Inspired by her, I started changing my prayer language. Instead of asking, "God, will You help me win this battle?" I began declaring, "Thank You, God, that victory is already mine in Christ."[36] I leaned on Scriptures like 1 Corinthians 15:57, which reminds me that through Christ, I'm "more than a conqueror." Now, every prayer session begins with gratitude for the victory

36 Rom. 8:37

already secured. It's not just semantics—it's a shift that rewires my heart to expect God's triumph.

Journaling the Journey

To keep this mindset alive, I started a victory journal. It's nothing fancy—just a notebook where I jot down every answered prayer, no matter how small. A kind word from a coworker, a moment of clarity in a tough decision, a bill paid just in time—these are all victories. Reviewing these entries during tough times reminds me of God's faithfulness. I've also begun sharing these stories with friends, and it's amazing how recounting God's goodness lifts everyone's spirits. It's like Esther's people fasting and praying together—our shared victories build a collective confidence in God's power.

Preparing with Peace

Esther's people didn't just pray; they prepared diligently, trusting God's plan. I've learned to approach challenges the same way. Whether it's a work project or a personal struggle, I make a plan, but I check my heart first. Am I preparing out of fear or faith? I speak life over my plans, affirming that they're guided by God's wisdom. This shift—from anxiety-driven striving to peace-filled preparation—has transformed how I face obstacles. It's not about avoiding challenges but about meeting them with the calm assurance that God is already at work.

Praising Before the Breakthrough

Cultivating a culture of praise has been a game-changer. I set reminders on my phone to pause and thank God for His victory, even in the middle of a hectic day. I've started worshipping in advance, praising God for outcomes before I see them. When challenges arise, my first response is to declare His goodness through a song or a simple "Thank You, Lord." It's like Esther and her people fasting with hope, not despair. Praise keeps my heart anchored in God's promises, no matter what I'm facing.

Surrounding Myself with Winners

I've also learned the importance of community. Esther didn't stand alone—she had Mordecai and her people. I've sought out faith-filled friends who share this victory mindset. We pray together, not just for our needs but to reinforce God's triumph in our lives. I've had to guard my circle, too, gently distancing myself from voices that stir up fear or doubt. It's not about judgment; it's about protecting the atmosphere where faith can thrive.

Seeing the Victory

Visualization has become a powerful tool. I take time each day to picture the breakthroughs God has promised—whether it's healing in a relationship or success in a new endeavor. I anchor these visions in Scriptures like Isaiah 54:17, which declares, "No weapon formed against you shall prosper." Speaking these truths aloud, I declare the victory as if it's already unfolding. This practice doesn't just build faith; it trains my mind to see God's hand at work.

Celebrating Every Step

One of the most joyful habits I've adopted is celebrating small wins. I used to wait for the "big" breakthroughs, but now I thank God for every step forward—a productive day, a moment of courage, a kind interaction. Each small win builds momentum, like stones in a foundation, strengthening my faith for the journey ahead.

Fighting with Peace

Esther didn't fight Haman with anger or manipulation; she trusted God's strategy. I've learned to refuse the temptation to fight back with fleshly weapons. Instead, I choose peace, letting the Holy Spirit guide my responses. When offenses come, I declare forgiveness quickly, keeping my heart aligned with heaven. This approach doesn't just defuse conflict—it positions me to walk in God's authority.

Holding Steady in Silence

There are seasons when victory feels distant, when prayers seem unanswered. Esther faced such moments, yet she stayed anchored. I've learned to hold the line in these quiet seasons by repeating God's Word until my spirit aligns. Consistency is key—daily prayer, worship, and declarations keep me grounded, even when I can't see the outcome.

Looking Beyond Myself

Finally, I've realized that victory isn't just for me. Like Esther, I'm called to advocate for others—my family, my church, my community. I pray for their breakthroughs and share my victories to inspire them. I want my life to leave a legacy, teaching the next generation to fight from a place of victory, not for it.

A Call to Action

Living in victory starts with a single step. I identified an area where I felt defeated—a lingering fear about my future. I crafted a decree based on Deuteronomy 20:4: "The Lord my God goes with me to fight for me against my enemies, to give me victory." For the past 30 days, I've spoken this aloud daily. The changes are subtle but real—a growing peace, a stronger trust. I'm tracking these shifts in my journal and sharing them with a friend to encourage her faith, too.

Reflection and Commitment

As I reflect, I ask myself: What Scriptures can I declare to strengthen my mindset? Who in my circle can help me stay anchored? What small wins can I celebrate today? And how is God prompting me to influence others through my victories? These questions keep me focused, while habits like weekly victory declarations, monthly testimony nights with friends, and quarterly fasting help me stay intentional.

Victory is not my destination; it's my starting point. What God decrees, no enemy can overturn. My voice enforces heaven's triumph on earth. Every act of faith establishes my authority, and joy and peace are the markers of this victorious life. Like Esther, I'm learning to live not for victory, but from it—every single day.

CHAPTER 10

REST AS A LEGACY

There remains a rest for the people of God.

HEBREW 4:9

The Institution of Purim: Celebration and Remembrance

Victory is not complete until it is remembered, and rest is not fully realized until it is integrated into the rhythms of our lives. Esther's complete victory is marked by Purim, a lasting celebration of God's deliverance intended to bring ongoing rest, joy, and remembrance to future generations.

Following their remarkable victory, Esther and Mordecai recognized the necessity of creating a rhythm of remembrance. They understood that without intention, even the most miraculous acts of God could fade into obscurity. Thus, they established Purim, an annual festival to honor how God transformed sorrow into joy and mourning into celebration.

The Scriptures state, "These days were to be remembered and observed in every generation by every family, and in every province and every city."[37] This decree ensured that the victory would endure in memory, grounding each new generation in the testimony of God's faithfulness.

Purim was a prophetic act. By commemorating what God had accomplished, the Jewish people were consistently reminded of their covenant identity and the power of their God. Each feast, gift exchange, and act of generosity proclaimed, "Our God delivers. Our God changes circumstances. Our God provides rest."

This principle is relevant for believers today. When God grants victory, it is vital to acknowledge it with remembrance. Celebrating deliverance reinforces it within our spirits, reminds us of God's power, and fortifies our faith for future challenges.

Esther's leadership in instituting Purim illustrates that rest is a deliberate choice. It involves pausing to celebrate, reflect, and express gratitude. Rest becomes a safeguard against forgetfulness and complacency, anchoring us in thankfulness and aligning us with God's ongoing work.

Moreover, Purim was inclusive, celebrated by all Jews, regardless of their status or location. This reflects God's heart: His victories are meant for the entire faith community, and His rest is accessible to all who seek Him. We are reminded that no one is beyond God's reach, and every believer is invited into rhythms of joy and rest.

Another significant aspect of Purim is its focus on generosity. Esther and Mordecai's decree encouraged the sharing of gifts and assistance to those in need. Rest and victory are not meant to end with us—they are intended to overflow. When God delivers us, we are called to be conduits of His goodness to others.

This outward perspective prevents victory from becoming self-serving and ensures our celebrations are characterized by compassion and community impact.

37 Est. 9:28

In practical terms, establishing rhythms of rest and remembrance might include:

- **Setting annual days of gratitude:** Celebrating anniversaries of significant breakthroughs with intentional observance and worship.
- **Creating family traditions:** Developing habits of storytelling and sharing testimonies to reinforce faith across generations.
- **Practicing generosity:** Using personal victories as opportunities to bless others in tangible ways.

The legacy of Purim serves as a model for weaving remembrance into the fabric of daily life, ensuring that God's goodness is never overlooked and that future generations grow with a profound awareness of His faithfulness.

Esther's story concludes with Mordecai rising to prominence and the Jewish community experiencing peace and security. This is the outcome of divine victory: not merely a singular breakthrough but a lasting legacy of rest, joy, and justice.

Next, we will explore how your victory extends beyond yourself—it becomes a blueprint for others, establishing enduring rhythms of faith, joy, and worship.

Rest Is Sustained Through Rhythm, Joy, and Memorials

Maintaining rest is rooted in rhythm. The Jewish tradition commands the celebration of Purim annually, creating a cycle of remembrance and joy. This rhythm nurtures their hearts and keeps their spirits alert. By establishing this pattern, they combat forgetfulness and continually reconnect with God's faithfulness, centering themselves amidst life's pressures.

You can cultivate your own spiritual rhythms by:

- **Setting aside a Sabbath rest:** Dedicate one day each week to rest and focus on God.

- **Practicing seasonal fasting:** Designate specific times to realign with God's purposes.
- **Creating annual gratitude markers:** Intentionally celebrate key breakthroughs and victories.

Rhythm acts as a safeguard, ensuring your spirit remains healthy and your faith vibrant. Without it, victories can fade, and spiritual lethargy may set in.

Joy is the second pillar of sustained rest. Purim is a festival of joy where the community feasts, exchanges gifts, and rejoices in God's deliverance. Joy transcends mere emotion; it is a spiritual discipline. As Nehemiah states, "the joy of the Lord is your strength."[38] Joy strengthens, uplifts, and drives us forward.

To foster joy:

- **Celebrate your victories:** Take time to enjoy and appreciate every breakthrough.
- **Practice daily gratitude:** Begin or end each day by listing things you are thankful for.
- **Share your joy:** Involve others in your celebrations through testimonies and acts of generosity.

Esther's community didn't celebrate in isolation; they included their families, neighbors, and even strangers in the festivities. Joy expands when shared, creating an environment where God's presence is palpable and His goodness is evident.

The third pillar is memorials. Memorials act as visible reminders of God's intervention. In the Old Testament, the Israelites built altars or erected stones to commemorate significant divine moments. These markers conveyed a message to future generations: "Here, God acted powerfully."

Purim itself serves as a living memorial. Each tradition, feast, and reading of the Esther scroll commemorates God's faithfulness, affirming, "We will not forget what God has done."

38 Neh. 8:10

You can create memorials in your life by:

- **Keeping a testimony journal:** Document every significant breakthrough.
- **Creating visual reminders:** Display meaningful symbols or artwork in your home that reflect God's faithfulness.
- **Sharing family stories:** Regularly recount stories of God's goodness with your children or loved ones.

These memorials act as anchors. When faced with new challenges, they remind you of God's unchanging nature and His proven record of deliverance.

Sustaining rest involves pausing to reflect, celebrate, and remember. It rejuvenates the spirit for future challenges. This practice, exemplified by Esther's thriving community, incorporates rest, joy, and memorials. It's easy to forget that our fast-paced world often overlooks these vital pauses.

Esther's legacy encourages us to embrace a deeper rhythm—one where every achievement is acknowledged, every joy is celebrated, and every deliverance is remembered. This is how rest transforms from a fleeting moment into a holistic way of life.

As we approach the conclusion of Esther's extraordinary narrative, we will examine how your victories and rhythms of rest can influence future generations, serving as a foundation and inheritance for them to experience God's faithfulness.

Your Victory Becomes Someone Else's Blueprint

When Esther and Mordecai established Purim, they did more than commemorate the past; they laid a foundation for the future. Each generation that celebrates Purim is reminded of how God uses ordinary individuals to achieve extraordinary deliverance. Esther's victory serves as a testament that God can and will intervene when His people act in faith and obedience.

This conveys a significant spiritual principle: your response to God today prepares the way for someone else's breakthrough tomorrow.

Your faith-filled "yes" becomes a guide for others facing similar challenges. Whether within your family, church, or community, the victories God brings through your life are intended to inspire, instruct, and empower others.

Esther's approach included several key elements that we can emulate:

- **Obedience in obscurity:** Esther's journey to influence began long before she became queen. Her quiet submission to Mordecai's guidance set the stage for her greater responsibilities. Your private victories are important and often lead to public successes.
- **Courage in crisis:** Esther's willingness to risk everything by approaching the king exemplifies timeless bravery. Each act of courage you demonstrate strengthens those observing your faith journey.
- **Rest in warfare:** Esther's purposeful waiting, her fast, and her reliance on God's timing illustrate the importance of fighting from a place of rest. This balance of boldness and patience becomes a vital lesson for those facing their own challenges.
- **Celebration and remembrance:** By establishing Purim, Esther and Mordecai ensured that future generations would remember God's faithfulness. Your testimony and celebrations remind others that God is always at work, even in unseen ways.

Sharing your victory blueprint can be as simple as recounting your testimony in small groups, mentoring someone new to faith, or documenting the steps God guided you through during a specific challenge. The aim is to transform your experiences into a source of strength and wisdom for others.

Esther's legacy teaches us that true victory multiplies when shared. It doesn't conclude with one person's success; it sparks a chain reaction of faith. This is how God's Kingdom grows—through testimonies that testify to His power and love.

It's also important to understand that your blueprint will differ from someone else's. Esther's journey was unique, but the principles of faith, obedience, and rest are universal. Encourage others to apply these principles in ways that align with their God-given assignments and seasons.

The beauty of legacy lies in transforming personal triumphs into collective strength. When you share your story, you become a foundational element in someone else's faith journey. Your victory conveys, "If God did it for me, He will do it for you."

As we conclude Esther's remarkable story, remember that our own stories, at any stage, can empower others. Our triumphs pave the way for future success.

In closing reflection, we will see how the legacy of Esther's anointing continues to empower believers today, demonstrating that rest, boldness, and surrender to God are timeless tools in the hands of God's people.

EPILOGUE

THE ESTHER ANOINTING IN OUR TIME

The story of Esther serves as more than just an ancient historical narrative; it acts as a guiding framework for contemporary believers facing challenges, opposition, and divine assignments today. The Esther anointing—a powerful combination of grace, courage, strategy, and rest—empowers God's people around the world. As we conclude this book, we are reminded that Esther's legacy endures, inspiring a new generation of hidden warriors to rise with boldness and spiritual authority.

Throughout history, God has raised up Esthers—individuals positioned in influential roles, both seen and unseen, for such a time as this. The Esther anointing is not exclusive to royalty or traditional leaders; it is available to every believer willing to align with divine purposes through surrender and faith.

We witness the Esther anointing when ordinary individuals embrace extraordinary assignments with humility and precision. It manifests in boardrooms and classrooms, homes, and mission fields. Wherever there is a need for divine intervention and righteous influence, God calls forth Esthers to make a difference.

This anointing encompasses several key characteristics:

- **Courageous Obedience:** Esther takes action even in the face of fear. They confront challenges with unwavering determination, recognizing that obedience is their highest form of worship.
- **Strategic Wisdom:** Like Esther, modern-day warriors seek God's guidance before proceeding. They appreciate the significance of timing, tone, and spiritual insight.
- **Grace-Filled Boldness:** The Esther anointing combines gentleness with strength. It is assertive without being abrasive, firm without being harsh. This balance attracts favor and creates opportunities.
- **Spiritual Rest:** Central to Esther's story is the theme of rest—a profound trust in God's sovereignty. Esthers are not driven by anxiety but by a deep-seated confidence that God is in control.

This anointing is urgently needed in today's world, which is rife with injustice, uncertainty, and evolving cultural landscapes. Nevertheless, God's promises remain steadfast, and His call to rise is unmistakable. The Esther anointing empowers believers to navigate these challenges with unwavering faith and transformative impact.

You may question your qualifications to carry this anointing. Esther herself grappled with feelings of unworthiness and fear regarding her assignment. Yet, God's grace covered her vulnerabilities, and His Spirit guided her actions. The same holds true for you. Your hidden seasons, quiet acts of deference, and willingness to seek God in stillness all prepare you for moments of divine purpose.

The Esther anointing is not merely a title; it is a way of life. It represents a commitment to live surrendered, pray fervently, act courageously, and rest deeply in God's plan. It is the choice to believe that your life holds divine significance, regardless of how ordinary your circumstances may seem.

As we observe, we see numerous believers stepping into their Esther moments—men and women advocating for justice, interceding quietly, leading with integrity, and standing firm against adversity. These modern-day Esthers remind us that God is continually at work, crafting redemption stories through those who yield to His will.

In conclusion, the Esther anointing invites you into a deeper partnership with God. It calls you to:

- Embrace hidden seasons as preparation.
- Seek divine strategies over human solutions.
- Step forward in bold obedience when God says, "Now."
- Rest assured that victory is assured.

May Esther's story continue to inspire you. May her example ignite renewed courage within you. And may you, too, rise with confident faith, knowing that God is still transforming circumstances, empowering hidden warriors, and fulfilling His promises through those who are willing to say yes.

Your Esther moment awaits.

REVIEW REQUEST FOR THE END OF THE BOOK

 **Thank You for Finishing This Journey**

We pray *Queen Esther: Spiritual Warfare from the Position of Rest* has spoken life, strategy, and peace into your spiritual walk.

If this book stirred something in your heart—encouraged, challenged, or empowered you—we kindly ask you to **leave a review on Amazon**. Your words can help others find truth, rest, and victory through Esther's story.

Visit this link to leave your review:

www.ingramcontent.com/pod-product-compliance
Lightning Source LLC
LaVergne TN
LVHW090521110826
845146LV00003B/939